THY WILL BE DONE

To Mark McIntosh, with gratitude,
respect and love.

THY WILL BE DONE

The 2021 Lent Book

Stephen Cherry

BLOOMSBURY CONTINUUM
LONDON · OXFORD · NEW YORK · NEW DELHI · SYDNEY

BLOOMSBURY CONTINUUM
Bloomsbury Publishing Plc
50 Bedford Square, London, WC1B 3DP, UK

BLOOMSBURY, BLOOMSBURY CONTINUUM and the Diana logo
are trademarks of Bloomsbury Publishing Plc

First published in Great Britain 2020

ISBN: PB: 978-1-4729-7825-7; eBook: 978-1-4729-7828-8;
ePDF: 978-1-4729-7827-1

2 4 6 8 10 9 7 5 3 1

Typeset by Deanta Global Publishing Services, Chennai, India
Printed and bound in Great Britain by CPI Group (UK) Ltd, Croydon CR0 4YY

To find out more about our authors and books visit www.bloomsbury.com
and sign up for our newsletters

CONTENTS

INTRODUCTION

This book is an invitation to immerse yourself in the prayer that Jesus taught his disciples.

We know it by heart. It has a good rhythmic structure; to recite it is effortless. We have said it in the silence of our hearts, and had it on our lips with others, whether in twos or threes or in congregations of tens or hundreds or thousands. We have said it in the babble of people praying the same prayer but each in their own mother tongue. We have heard it on great national occasions broadcast from St Paul's Cathedral or Westminster Abbey. It is the Lord's Prayer, the 'Our Father', and for a Christian it is the prayer of prayers.

For the last six years I have led the saying of this prayer at the Festival of Nine Lessons and Carols from King's College, Cambridge, where I am Dean of Chapel. The thousand people in the building who have said it along with me have all been aware of the millions of people joining in as they listen in from around the world. At another extreme, there have been countless times when, stuck for words in a situation of intimacy and sadness such as a deathbed, I have just started up with 'Our Father, who art in heaven …' and found the words taking hold of the moment, deepening the fellowship and offering solace and hope. My experiences may be vividly extreme, but they point to a common truth. The Lord's Prayer is often the first place we look for spiritual support both in the most public and the most private parts of our lives.

While not a poem, the Lord's Prayer has a richly poetic quality. To engage in it is to be drawn into something we understand, to a degree, but also know that we cannot quite fathom. It is also to be drawn into relationship with the countless others who have come across these words, used them as their own, and found in them both meaning and mystery. When we read, recite or learn a good and genuine poem we are also drawn into relationship with the author. Real poems come from the depths and engaging with them seriously gives us access to the soul of the poet as well as their perceptions, priorities and responses. In the same way, perhaps, praying the Lord's Prayer will draw us into a deeper relationship with its originator, Jesus himself, as well as with the countless others who have used and reflected on the prayer.

The Lord's Prayer's poetic quality is not something incidental to its nature or its power. It is a short collection of words that is so rich in meaning and with such a capacious heart that we can find a home in it for deep feelings and fresh thoughts. It is also a springboard for inspired practical action – for the deeds and activities that make up our daily lives.

The chapters that follow offer encounters not only with the words of the prayer but with some of the many who have commented on it, taught about it, interpreted it or been inspired by it down the ages. A very great deal has been written. This is in part because, as the Anglican bishop and scholar, Kenneth Stevenson, has put it, the prayer is 'richly ambiguous'. I think I know what he means, but that isn't quite the phrase I'd use. Certainly there are a number of riddles in the prayer that cannot be resolved by scholarship, but I think that the intrigue of these conundrums can sometimes focus the attention in ways that are a little narrower and more detailed than is helpful. Step back a little and the richness and depth of the prayer resolve into something clear, hopeful and inspiring about the relationship between God and humanity that all prayer seeks to animate and sustain. Personally, I find more challenge than ambiguity, but ultimately more guidance than challenge.

Reflective immersion in the prayer, perhaps itself a way of praying it, will also draw us closer to the mind and heart of Jesus Christ; indeed, it might draw us towards that most profound aspect of who Jesus was and is – his relationship with his own heavenly Father. It is right and wise, I believe, to be hesitant to speak of that relationship, recognizing that this, of all realities, is likely to be beyond our comprehension. We can perhaps speculate, however, that there are times when that relationship was more than usually the focus of Jesus' attention. These would include his withdrawal to the wilderness after he was baptized, and the various acts in which he gradually took leave of his disciples before his passion, in particular the Last Supper and his agonized prayer in the Garden of Gethsemane. To these may be added the occasions when he slipped away from his companions to a quiet place to pray alone. We might well wonder what went on during those times of sacred solitude. There are no records, but it might not be mere speculation to suggest that whatever he took into prayer it was what we call the Lord's Prayer that ultimately emerged.

According to Luke, it was after Jesus returned from one of his brief retreats that one of his disciples asked him for a lesson in prayer. He responded by giving them what we might now call 'a form of words'. Matthew introduces his longer version of the prayer rather differently. It is presented right at the heart of the Sermon on the Mount, a compilation of Jesus' words of teaching given without any details of context or what might have prompted them. For those who feel that an invitation to pray is an invitation to be pious or to make a performance of their spirituality or morality, the words of Jesus are a chillingly cold shower, stressing that it is wrong to allow piety in any form – he singles out praying and giving alms – to become a sort of self-presentation; such posturing is denounced as hypocrisy – just playing a role.

According to Jesus, our prayer is to be an act of sincerity offered for its own sake; behind closed doors rather than out in the street. He castigates the Gentiles who 'heap up empty phrases' because 'they think they will be heard because of their many words'. There is no point in this because 'your Father knows what you need before you ask him' (Matthew 6.7-8). Whatever else prayer might be, it is neither an opportunity to impress others nor one to provide God with information. This is Jesus' most fundamental lesson about prayer. Only when it has been grasped can we graduate to hearing, and making our own, the words that he then shared, which we now call the Lord's Prayer.

Immersion in the Lord's Prayer, then, might come at something of a cost. In particular, to get more deeply into the prayer that Jesus taught we may have to let go of some of our assumptions about prayer and habits of praying. Boiling Jesus' advice down to its essence, we might advise ourselves to have fewer words, less ego and less anxiety in our prayer. That is, to make it simpler.

We might also make it lighter. Prayer, wrongly understood, can seem like a burden, a weight, a responsibility. But there is no sense of heaviness in Jesus' teaching about prayer. 'Don't get too wound up about it,' is his message, 'just say this ...' Put that way it sounds very easy indeed. And yet such a suggestion of ease in prayer might itself make us feel uneasy. Surely our prayer must have not only sincerity, but also weight, heft, seriousness, gravitas. And, depending on the specifics of your spiritual snobbery, you may feel that a true prayer must have either sophisticated grammar or intense emotion. Such feelings are, however, an indication that we have wandered far from Jesus' teaching and have alienated ourselves from God's love and grace more than we realize. 'My yoke is easy,' said Jesus, 'and my burden is light' (Matthew 11.30). Of course it doesn't always feel like that, but when the burden weighs heavily it might be that the problem is not with the yoke or the burden, but with us. Maybe we make heavier weather of prayer than we need. Maybe it's *meant* to be effortless, easy and light.

Simplicity and lightness in prayer are not the same as naivety or glibness. Although Jesus gives us a 'form of words', as I put it, the warning against 'empty phrases' persists. The Lord's Prayer can be valid for us even when we are not fully mindful of all its nuances or implications but are being taken along by its familiarity, its rhythms and the fact that other people are saying it, or that we have now got to the point in the service where it is usually said and so join in the words while our busy mind worries about other matters or wanders off on its own. But being 'taken along' does not represent maturity in prayer or the end of our spiritual journey into the praying heart of Jesus. So, while delighting in the simplicity and lightness of the Lord's Prayer, we need also, I suggest, to de-familiarize ourselves from it so that we may discover its challenges and deeper mysteries.

The intention of this book, then, is to facilitate an extended immersion in the prayer that Jesus taught us so that we might pray it more profoundly. To do this we need both to embrace the 'easiness' of the prayer and to overcome its over-familiarity. If we can manage both we may come to appreciate anew the prayer's eternal freshness.

The book is divided into six parts, all of which focus on one clause of the prayer. Each part consists of six chapters. This means that the book can work both as an exploration of the Lord's Prayer that may be engaged with at any time, and as a Lent Book that provides short daily readings, six days a week, from the Sunday before Ash Wednesday to the Sunday after Easter Day.

PART ONE

HEAVEN

Our Father, who art in heaven, hallowed be thy name;

If we call our Father Him who is incorruptible and just and good, we must prove by our life that the kinship is real.

Gregory of Nyssa

I

THE SHAPE OF THE PRAYER

Our immersion in the Lord's Prayer begins with
a look at the version found in Matthew's Gospel.
Offered as part of Jesus' teaching about how to pray,
these 57 Greek words are the basis of the prayer that
we know and use today. We can't really say that this
is the 'original' version, partly because Jesus didn't
use Greek. He spoke in Aramaic, so even authentic
quotations in the original Gospels are translations.
Nonetheless, what we have in Matthew is the closest
biblical text to what we call the Lord's Prayer today
and it is instructive to consider it. We will do that, not
by putting the New Testament Greek on the page here,
but by considering a literal translation of Matthew's
words (Matthew 6.9-13). That will provide more
than enough de-familiarization to get us started.

Father of us the one in the heavens,
let be revered the name of you,

let come the kingdom of you,
let be done the will of you,
as in heaven also on earth.
The bread of us daily give us today.
And forgive us the debts of us,
as also we have forgiven the debtors of us.
And do not bring us into temptation,
but rescue us from the evil one.

Several points are immediately apparent. The first is the phrase 'of you' that concludes lines two, three and four and then disappears completely. This repetition makes very clear something that is maybe hidden by more fluent translations. Namely, that the Lord's Prayer falls into two halves and that the first half is all about God. In particular, it's about God's 'fatherhood', 'name', 'kingdom' and 'will'.

For those of us who think that the fundamental form of prayer is 'Dear God, please would you …?' or 'Loving Father, you really ought to know that …', the Lord's Prayer is something of a shock. There is no ask here, nor is there confession. The first half of the Lord's Prayer is affirmation of God and God's intentions. This is where Jesus wants us to begin when we pray: not with ourselves – but with God. If asked to paraphrase the first half of the prayer, we might say: 'Our God, we acknowledge that you are holy and that you have a purpose – and we assent to both.'

Turning now to the second half of the prayer, we might observe that it is very different in style. We are indeed back down to earth with a bump. Jesus bids us ask for daily bread, for forgiveness, to be spared temptation and rescued from the evil one.

Jesus also requires us to connect our prayer for forgiveness with our own forgiveness of others. There is a lot going on here and it is, inevitably, far more than a wish-list of our wants, needs, desires, or, for that matter, a worry-list of our uppermost concerns and anxieties. The second half of the prayer is harder to paraphrase, but if we put the tricky forgiveness clause to one side for a moment (don't worry, we will certainty return to it), we could summarize it as: 'Give us what we need, and keep us away from everything that may harm us.'

So – a prayer of two halves. Are you convinced? What I have presented here could be described as a very 'Western' analysis of the prayer. Western theologians have often subdivided the two halves (actually the word 'tables' is sometimes used to describe the two halves) by identifying three 'heavenly petitions' in the first and four 'earthly petitions' in the second. The Eastern or Orthodox view, however, doesn't see the prayer as being divided into two halves and identifies only six different petitions, as it conflates 'lead us not into temptation' with 'but deliver us from evil'.

If you look closely at the contents of this book, you will see that I have followed neither pattern here, as I only have six sections, including the words that don't appear in the Bible but that have been used as a fitting conclusion since earliest times, 'for thine is the kingdom, the power and the glory for ever and ever. Amen.' The effect of including these words is to create both progression and symmetry. The prayer begins with God's 'fatherhood' and ends with God's glory. And in between it is focused on three facets of human lived experience – our needs in the present, our relationship with what has gone wrong in the past, and our fears for the future.

2

MOTHERLY FATHER

The question of how to begin a prayer confronts everyone who has ever sought to pray. Jesus was a person of prayer long before he taught his disciples to pray, and we can be sure that as he prayed he drew on the prayers of the Bible – not least the great collection of poetic biblical prayers called the Psalms. We might expect, therefore, that when Jesus did teach his disciples to pray, he would have put forward a familiar image or idea from that basic repertoire of prayer. The surprise is that he did not. The word with which the prayer begins is not 'Judge' or 'Lord' or 'Master' or 'Mighty One' or even 'Almighty', but 'Father'.

It would be wrong to imagine that Jesus was here inviting people to think of their own relationship with their male parent and then extend that to their relationship with God. There is no evidence that he had a particularly high regard for his earthly father and he certainly took the opportunity from time to time to distance himself from the idea that the domestic or genetic unit was especially important (Matthew 12.48-50). For Jesus and his Jewish followers the duty to respect parents, and to care for them when they became needy, was enshrined in the Commandment: 'Honour thy father and thy mother.' But for Jesus our duty of care is far more extensive than an exclusive focus on the family.

When Jesus used the word 'Father' as the mode of address with which to begin this prayer, he was shifting the focus of our relationship with God from one based on power and deference to one based on care and support. When we pray to the 'Father' we pray to the one who caused us to be and sustains us in life, not to one who owns us as a subject or who has power over us that we fear will be exercised harshly, or who matters primarily because it is by them that we are held to account for our thoughts, words and deeds. The 'Father' whom Jesus addresses is not a potentate who terrifies, but a progenitor who is deeply benevolent.

It's also important to appreciate that when Jesus used the word that we translate as 'Father', he was not making a definitive statement to the effect that God is more like your father than any other person you can think of or imagine. Nor was he saying that your earthly father is the best model of God that can ever be suggested. And he was certainly not saying that 'your father is more important than your mother'. On the contrary, he was deliberately moving people's understanding of God from the institutional to the relational. That, as time has gone by, it is the father of the household who has been taken to embody and represent a more formal, discipline-oriented figure than has the mother is, given Jesus' choice of words, the source of significant confusion. The biblical scholar Joachim Jeremias understood this point well and addressed it by writing that 'the word "Father", as applied to God, thus encompasses, from earliest times, something of what the word "Mother" signifies among us'.

Writing much more recently, the Jesuit priest and leading Catholic theologian Gerald O'Collins – seeking to capture here the sense of forgiveness seen in the father of the prodigal son, Jesus' compassion for the large hungry crowd that gathered to hear him, and his uses of the imagery of a mother hen caring for her chicks under her wings to describe his mission – suggested that the God to whom Jesus prays might be thought of as a 'motherly father'. The origin of the bird and wings imagery is found in the Old Testament, but, according to O'Collins, not only did Jesus apply to himself imagery used for God but he also 'gave the image a very homely twist by representing himself not as a mighty eagle but as a barnyard hen'. O'Collins goes on to expound the 'motherly father' phrase in terms of the way in which the death and resurrection is presented by the evangelists and, in particular, by a sequence in the Gospel of John. It is John who uses the metaphor of childbirth to explain the paroxysm of pain and lamentation that accompanies the birthing of a new way and how it is all swallowed by joy. It is John, too, who names the women who stand as silent witnesses to the crucifixion, and Mary Magdalene as the bewildered and distressed witness to the resurrection. O'Collins sees this as a 'feminine sequence' that has a deeper symbolic meaning – one perhaps not evident to the writer. 'It may prove hard to catch this meaning in a net of words, but we should not bypass the task of reflecting on the feminine face of Jesus' death, burial and resurrection – a face which also lets us glimpse some characteristics of the God whom Jesus preached and revealed.'

The figure of Mary, the mother of Jesus, not only runs through this narrative, and indeed the whole gospel narrative right up to and including Pentecost, but also hovers over it as the Virgin Mary or 'Our Lady'. Oddly, 'Our Lady' is not often connected to the 'Our Father', but might it be that there is in the deep spirituality of this prayer an integration of two principles that Christianity has done well to retain, but perhaps done too much to hold apart? Carl Jung, one of the founders of psychoanalysis, and the unwitting progenitor of the Myers–Briggs personality testing industry, believed that the doctrine of the Assumption of Mary was 'the most important religious event since the Reformation' because it signified that the feminine principle had been absorbed into the Godhead.

Certainly, those who meditate on or pray with Andrei Rublev's great fifteenth-century icon of the Trinity, based on the hospitality of Abraham, will be struck by the feminine nature of the forms and the androgyny of the faces. There can be no doubt that had Rublev wanted to depict God as a bearded man he would have had the resources to do so – and countless examples to follow. But he didn't. Another image that points to the way in which masculine and feminine principles are held together in the divine, as Henri Nouwen observed, is found in the different forms of the two hands of the forgiving father in Rembrandt's masterpiece *The Return of the Prodigal*.

These two images are today reproduced thousands if not millions of times each year. Maybe part of their power is that they communicate something integrating and healthy and complete about the understanding of God's nature and of God's relationship with us. There are many people for whom that health and fullness is no longer conveyed by the word 'father' alone, while for others the word is still able to do its spiritual work of connecting muddled human beings with the God of comprehensive and all-encompassing love. Whatever we say, however, when we use the word 'father' here we are implying 'mother' and referring to the loving-kindness of God.

3

OUR FATHER

One of the many notable aspects of this prayer is that is it *not* written in the first person. It is not *my* father who is prayed to, but *our* father. This is a significant contrast with the biblical prayers that would have shaped Jesus' own spirituality, as well as being a serious challenge to the way we often think about ourselves and God today.

According to Matthew, Mark and Luke, Jesus dies with words from the Psalms on his lips. In Luke his dying words are, 'Into your hand I commit my spirit' (Psalm 31.5). In Matthew and Mark it is this harrowing phrase: 'My God, my God why have you forsaken me?' (Psalm 22.1). The two verses convey very different sentiments and attitudes, but in one regard they are the same. They are spoken in the first person. *I* commit *my* spirit, and why hast thou forsaken *me*?

In the prayer that Jesus taught, however, there is no 'I'. It is all 'our': 'our Father', and later 'our bread' and 'our sins'. It is not about 'me'; it is all about 'us'.

The reality is that whenever we pray as Jesus taught us, we cannot get away from everyone else. Others, very many others, are always implicitly present as soon as we start the prayer, 'Our Father ...' It's as if the prayer puts a condition in front of us. If you want to relate to God, you must also relate to others. For those who have read the earlier part of the Sermon on the Mount, this should come as no surprise. A huge amount of it concerns human relationships. And this is in turn consistent with the summary of the law: love God and love your neighbour as yourself (Matthew 22.37-39), and with the verses that come at the climax of the sermon in which the disciples are invited to love even those who have hostile intent towards them – their enemies (Matthew 5.44).

By being earthed and grounded not in 'my' but in 'our', and not in 'I' but in 'us' – that is, not in individuality but in community – the Lord's Prayer offers a profound challenge to the liberal individualism that so often frames experience and meaning today, together with our understanding of what a good life looks like. The focus of this prayer is absolutely not on the praying individual and their self-identified projects for fulfilment. Taking it seriously steers us away from the existential conclusion of the seventeenth-century French philosopher and mathematician René Descartes that 'I think therefore I am.' On the contrary, if and as we let the Lord's Prayer shape us, we will find that the barriers around the self begin to dissolve and we begin to discover our true identity not as 'me' but as a member of a broad communion of people who belong to each other through God.

There is, of course, a question of inclusion here. Who are the 'others' we have in mind when we say 'our'? How far does this 'communion' extend? We might think of several different answers. First, those who are sharing in the prayer at the same time. Second, those who share in the prayer at any time. Third, those who have deliberately and intentionally committed themselves to Christian faith. Fourth, it might extend to all human beings.

This is the way I have come to understand it: we refer to God as 'our Father' not because we feel that 'we' are a distinct and separate family, but because God is the Father of all and because our relationship to God is based not on our decision or action but on God's grace. We think of God as 'ours' because

God made us and God loves us – all. The 'our' in the Our Father is only limited by the constraints of our imagination, which is precisely what the prayer seeks to challenge and enlarge. Just as the boundaries of the self are dissolved as we repeatedly pray 'our', so our sense of community and fellowship with others is expanded as we imagine those who are saying it with us. So, even if we start with the first suggestion above (the 'our' refers to those in the gathered group who are praying together), praying the prayer will sooner or later transport us to the fourth – the understanding that God is the 'motherly Father' of all humanity.

4

THE PROBLEM OF PATRIARCHY

Writing about this in the first quarter of the twenty-first century, it is natural to feel the force of a question that would have been far from the mind of the one who taught us this prayer. Is the Lord's Prayer, in its very opening, a patriarchal prayer? And if so, does that vitiate the power and undermine the purpose of the prayer from the outset? Those are general questions, but we might also want to ask a more specific one. Is the Lord's Prayer toxic for those who have experienced from their own father not support, love, care and encouragement, but harshness, bullying or abuse?

We have already noticed that theologians have seen in Jesus' use of the word 'father' an embrace of what we might think of as feminine qualities and the sort of parenting that has often been the domain of the mother. To take that a step further, we could say that no gender is implied by the word 'father'. We now appreciate more than ever that gender is a cultural phenomenon, a 'construction'. Nonetheless, the division of labour of two parents often falls along predictable lines. And it is often those who do the mothering who, like all who spend their time caring for others, are economically less valued.

None of this means that when we address God as Father we are adding an especial layer of value to the sorts of things that male parents do in comparison with those that female parents do. As we have seen, when Jesus called God 'Father' rather than 'Lord', the intention was not to elevate the status of fathers as opposed to mothers, but to reference a relationship of intimacy and dependency.

This is of small comfort to those for whom 'father' is a bad, sad or even toxic word. All language is potentially infected by sin, and liable to be corrupted by negative experiences. The argument that when Jesus used the word 'Father' he was softening the image of God in people's hearts is of no comfort to a victim of paternal abuse, whether that be the abuse of neglect, or mental, physical or sexual abuse. The issue is absolutely real, but it might also be one that cannot be fully resolved in the public use of the prayer.

An example might help us see this in context. In the English-speaking world it is rare indeed to come across a person whose name is Jesus. It is, however, relatively common in Spanish-speaking countries. I sometimes wonder whether there is among Spanish-speaking Christians a debate as to whether or not one can relate to Jesus of Nazareth as a person of loving-kindness if as a child you were bullied by the 'Jesús' who lived down the street, or if your husband 'Jesús' is cruel, or your boss 'Jesús' is a tyrant. I appreciate that this example doesn't deal with all the problems associated with patriarchy, but it does perhaps remind us that all language is vulnerable to the corruption of associations that can accrue over time.

Prayer may be the pursuit of purity and be addressed to the most perfect One, but it will always be using language that is impure and imperfect. The language will sometimes let us down and mislead us, and sometimes stand between us and the true spirit of the prayer. We must acknowledge this and make our peace with it both individually and as a community of praying people. Words that are intended to be helpful and comforting will sometimes be experienced as hurtful and alienating. Together, we need to understand this and live with this reality, being adept at changing our language when necessary but accommodating our sensibilities when change is not realistic; otherwise we will be undermining the loving and protective acceptance that words such as 'father' are intended to convey.

5

WHO ART IN HEAVEN

Heaven can be a problematic word today, especially if we think of it as the place where God is. Despite my theological training, sometimes I find it hard to get beyond the imagery of an old man sitting way above the clouds when I hear the phrase 'who art in heaven'. And yet I know perfectly well that whatever heaven is, it is not a location above the stratosphere. I also know that God does not and cannot approximate to any image I have of God, still less to a cliché of a grey-bearded grandfather, whether kindly or stern. But even a theologian as great and sophisticated as Karl Barth, the giant of twentieth-century Protestant theology, can write a phrase like, 'He is in heaven, on his throne' adding a grand chair to my already unrealistic and unhelpful mental image.

However, Barth doesn't really want to clog up my imagination with such images. His true intent is to explain to me that the word 'heaven' in this context is a reference to God's transcendence. Heaven for Barth isn't just an idea; it is real. It is 'part of the created world'. That is, it has its origin in God. And yet heaven is manifestly not part of this world. Nor is it something we can imagine. It is 'unapproachable and incomprehensible'. For Barth, God is not so much 'in heaven' as 'beyond heaven'. God is super-transcendent, one might say. Whatever 'container' you construct or imagine for God, God will elude it. Whatever you think of as 'beyond' – well, God is beyond that.

Some people find talk of incomprehensibility and beyond-ness to be comforting. Perhaps it connects with and affirms their inner mystic. For others it is an invitation to engage in abstract thought and argument. It stimulates the philosopher within. For Barth, however, neither of these is the right response. For him, 'God's transcendence is demonstrated, revealed, and actualized in Jesus Christ, who is the profundity of his omnipotent mercy.' Just when it seems that the words of the prayer are taking us to the heights of abstraction, Barth says 'no' and seeks to bring us down to the earthly life of the person Jesus, the incarnate word of God, with a very real bump. And so he leads me to understand that the word 'heaven' here does not invite me to put my head in, or even through, the clouds.

It's vital to remember that God, while 'other' to us, is not distant from us, but close. The God to whom we pray is not remote but intimate. As Augustine wrote in his famous *Confessions* in the fourth century: 'God is nearer to us than we are to ourselves', and as our Muslim siblings know from their scripture: 'we are closer to God than [his] jugular vein' (Qur'an 50.16).

A different aspect of the meaning and significance of 'heaven' comes from Thomas Aquinas, the great theologian of the twelfth century. For Aquinas, 'heaven' does not so much refer to transcendence as to *power*. As such, the reference to 'heaven' in the prayer is a source of great encouragement and hope to the one who prays. We express our need, and place our trust, not in an impotent image or idol, but in one who really can help. Aquinas's view is that such power is already vouched for when we refer to God as 'Father', but as he put it, 'lest there should be doubt concerning the perfection of his power, we add *who art in heaven*'. For Aquinas, the notion of finality as well as perfection is also implied by the word 'heaven' here: 'because our final happiness is not here on earth but in heaven'. That is, not in a certain distant place, but in the fulfilment of all our desires in the intimacy of God and the communion of God's people.

Between them, Karl Barth and Thomas Aquinas have taken us a long way from any naive image of God as an enthroned old man way up in the clouds. They lead us to understand that when we pray to God in heaven, we pray to one who is intimately present and personally powerful.

6

HALLOWED BE THY NAME

This is a particularly challenging phrase to people of today's world for two separate reasons. First, because the word 'hallowed' is unusual and obscure. It refers to 'holiness', which may sound a more familiar word but is also not a widely understood notion today. Second, because we don't think about names in the same way now as people did in Jesus' time and culture.

The background idea of holiness is that of different-ness or deliberate set-apartness. God is holy, by definition (so to speak), but other things and people can be made holy, typically by cultic acts and rituals. At least some acts of blessing render what is blessed to be 'holy'; the water used at baptism is a good example.

For the people of Israel, God's holy people, who were chosen, set apart and treated differently, it is God's law that, second to God, is the most holy thing conceivable. The law made the people holy because it is a reflection of the mind of God. And yet, as a whole string of prophets attested, the people violated their own holiness by straying from the law. This is why they were called to repent, that is, to return to holiness. John the Baptist continued this message, but also pointed beyond it to the saving holiness of Jesus Christ. 'Among you stands one whom you do not know, the one who is coming after me; I am not worthy to untie the thong of his sandal' (John 1.26-27). And: 'Here is the Lamb of God who takes away the sin of the world! This is he of whom I said, "After me comes a man who ranks ahead of me because he was before me"' (John 1.29-30). Paul the apostle, who adapted the prophetic call to repent to the evangelical call to the Gentiles, understood that those who responded and followed became 'holy ones' or, as it is often translated, 'saints'.

Holiness, then, is a word that refers to the extent to which something shows or represents God-like-ness. And yet in the Lord's Prayer it is not a material thing or a person that is to be hallowed, but God's *name* that is rendered holy. Clearly we need to think a bit more about names.

It is unfortunate that we have come to think of names as labels – a short string of sounds or letters that are meaningless apart from the fact that they refer to something. We need such names, or nouns, in order to live in a world of objects without confusion and chaos, and yet we also know that the same thing can have different names and that some names are more specific and helpful than others. We can ask for salt to put on our egg and chips, but there are situations where we should be more precise and say that it is sodium chloride that we seek. However, whether we say 'salt' or 'sodium chloride', the material to which we refer is the same white, crystalline and soluble stuff. The name doesn't make any difference; it really is just a label.

When we pray that God's name be hallowed, however, we are not talking about the 'name' of God as if it were a label. A name in this context is not the string of letters or sounds that refers to someone or something, but a way in which a person or thing is made especially present or real. There is a hint of this in our use of the word where a person's name (good or bad) is in fact their reputation. Just to mention a person of good standing and reputation can be to ennoble a gathering, elevate the tone of a discussion and heighten people's aspirations. Good reputations may not always be fully deserved, but this does not diminish their power.

When it comes to God, biblical culture is very reluctant indeed to dare to refer to God by an actual name. God, it turns out, is far too holy to have a name, and so 'name' itself becomes a circumlocution for 'God'.

Does this mean that the prayer is an otiose request, a petition that the most holy one *become* holy? Wouldn't that be like praying for sodium chloride to become salty?

Not at all.

To recite 'hallowed be thy name' is not to put a halo behind the word 'God' or 'father', but to do something quite different. It is to recognize that God's holiness is not a magic power, but a relational reality. God's holiness is intrinsic to God, but it only impacts on us when we acknowledge and respond to it. We recognize in saying these words that the holiness of God is indeed an apartness from us unless and until we respond to it affirmatively. A more helpful translation might therefore be 'may we recognize and respond to your holiness'.

The twentieth-century French philosopher, activist and mystic, Simone Weil, wrote that, 'This name is holiness itself; there is no holiness outside it; it does not therefore have to be hallowed. In asking for its hallowing we are asking for something which exists eternally, with full and complete reality, so that we can neither increase nor diminish it, even by an infinitesimal fraction.' And she continues to make the point that to ask for that which exists, 'really, infallibly, eternally, quite apart from our prayer ...' is not absurd or redundant or a waste of time and effort. Far from it. It is, she writes, the 'perfect petition'.

When we say 'hallowed be thy name', we affirm both the reality of God's goodness and perfection and their claim on our allegiance. And as we do so, we allow ourselves to be drawn towards that complete holiness that is uniquely found in God.

The Lord's Prayer is not a spell. And these words are not based on the vain thought that if I say the right thing, God's holiness will in some way be enhanced. Rather, they are words that, when I say them, put me in the position of one who is acknowledging the ultimate holiness of God, and willingly subjecting myself to the influence of that holiness. It is a prayer not that God's reputation be enhanced, but that I, or rather we, may be changed by recognizing and affirming it.

PART TWO

EARTH

Thy kingdom come; thy will be done;
on earth as it is in heaven.

The end and purpose of the world is the coming of the kingdom.

Karl Barth

7

ON EARTH AS IT IS IN HEAVEN

As we saw in the earlier chapters, the opening words of the prayer deliberately draw our minds and our hearts to the holiness and transcendence of God – at the same time as insisting that God is a 'motherly father' to us all. They invite us to imagine and engage with God, while at the same time indicating that God is utterly beyond anything we might have experienced or could ever imagine.

The second part of the prayer immediately takes us in a different direction. Its meaning is not controlled by its opening words, but by the phrase with which it concludes, 'on earth as it is in heaven'. If the first clause had us looking beyond ourselves in an upward direction, this one has us looking not down but around and about ourselves more horizontally.

If anyone had thought that Christian prayer should involve disengagement with everyday life or the pain of the world, this second sentence is a quick corrective.

Our prayer may – indeed should – have a meditative aspect, a contemplative dimension, and might even sometimes open us to blissful or mystical experiences. Indeed, if our prayers don't allow us to participate in joyful worship then nothing will. But in this particular and primary case, we are *not* invited to take our hearts and minds away from the realities of this world, but to engage with them in a re-energized way.

The 'this-worldly' focus of the Lord's Prayer is even more apparent if we turn our attention away from the familiar version based, as we have seen, on words in Matthew's Gospel and consider Luke's shorter version (Luke 11.2-4). In word-for-word translation, it reads like this:

> Father, let be held in reverence the name of you.
> Let come the kingdom of you.
> The bread of us daily give to us each day.
> And forgive the sins of us,
> for indeed [we] ourselves are forgiving everyone being indebted to us.
> And may you not lead us into temptation.

Faced with two versions of the same thing, one short and the other long, biblical scholars always ask which came first. Is the shorter version an edited version of the longer, or is the longer one an expanded version of the shorter? The scholarly consensus is that Luke's is likely to be the older version and that Matthew's is an expanded form. This doesn't mean that we know with any certainty that it approximates more closely to what Jesus said, or that all the words and phrases that are to be found in the long version, but not the short one, were Matthew's additions. We might, however, look to Luke's shorter and older version for a sense of what is more basic and fundamental about the prayer.

When we do look at it in that way, we see a direct prayer to the Father that, after the briefest of introductions, seeks God's kingdom, daily bread, mutual forgiveness and the desire to be spared temptation. There is no reference to heaven or to God's will and there is no request to be delivered from evil.

Luke's version is a very this-worldly prayer. This is clear. So is Matthew's, but it is less obvious, though the 'additions' do not change the focus of concern; they merely place it more firmly in the dual context that we explored in Part One: God's benevolent and intimate power and our fundamental and theological connectedness with others.

Matthew's is generally, therefore, the better prayer for us to use, provided that we do not let the theologically elevated language distract us from the compelling personal invitation to each one of us to engage with the prayer's earthly agenda. Returning to Luke from time to time might well assist us in this way and get us back down to earth.

Yes, earth! The phrase 'on earth as it is in heaven' might at first sight seem to be referring to those aspects of life on earth that are the most wholesome, pleasant, positive, delightful; the most heavenly or heaven-like experiences. In fact, the opposite is true. When we pray for the coming of God's kingdom or the doing of God's will 'on earth as it is in heaven', we are acknowledging and drawing attention to the *gap* between how things would be if God's will were done and God's kingdom had come and the way life actually is now in our experiences, in our communities and in our politics.

As we pray the Lord's Prayer, we put ourselves into that gap – the very place where Jesus lived and ministered, taught and healed, the space in which he suffered and died. Does that sound odd? We like to think that prayer might teleport us to heaven so that we can escape the pain and injustice of this world.

More often it sensitizes us to the pain of the world, attunes us to its realities and empowers us to respond.

A recent example of the Lord's Prayer being connected with a very earthly, but nonetheless symbolic matter comes from South Carolina. Herself the descendant of slaves, Brittany 'Bree' Newsome responded to the murder of nine parishioners who were attending a Bible study in Charleston in June 2015 by climbing the flagpole in front of the South Caroline Statehouse and removing the confederate flag. 'You come against me with hatred and oppression, and violence,' she shouted, atop her perilous pulpit with the flag in her hand. 'I come against you in the name of God. This flag comes down today.' The artist and daughter of a Baptist minister was risking her life to remove a symbol of white supremacy.

As Bree had climbed her way to the top of the flagpole, she had recited the twenty-seventh psalm, which begins, 'The LORD is my light and my salvation; whom shall I fear?', and the Lord's Prayer. She was arrested and the flag quickly replaced. However, she was released after a few hours and by the end of the same week the flag had been permanently removed. Since then, many other confederate memorials have been removed from public spaces.

Newsome's action meant 'No confederate flag on that bit of earth', reflecting her faith that there is no slavery in heaven. Racism persists, as we know, pervading human hearts and minds and embedded in structures, institutions, economic systems and all the other realities that together make up what we mean by 'earth'. When we pray for the coming of God's kingdom, we pray positively for the advance of all that is good, but there is a negative prayer too – for the decline and removal of all that is evil. 'This flag comes down today' means 'racism must be banished from the earth'. This is where the Lord's Prayer takes us. Indeed, it takes us a step further, from 'must be banished' to 'will be banished'. The phrase 'on earth as it is in heaven' is seen as both an imperative and a promise.

8

GOD'S KINGDOM

Jesus never defined anything. That wasn't his style or tradition. But of all the things that we might have wished he had defined, the 'kingdom of God' would come near the top of many people's lists.

He often spoke about the kingdom, but most of what he said about it was indirect. 'The kingdom of heaven is like …' he would begin, and thereafter tell a parable. He taught us that the kingdom of heaven was like a grain of mustard that was very small but the basis of a great bush that provided a habitat for birds. He said that it is like a woman who had lost a coin and obsessed about it until she found it. He likened it to a pearl of great price. And so it went on.

A huge amount of scholarship has focused on questions about the kingdom of God in recent decades. One of the reasons for this is that, in the twentieth century, theologians began to appreciate more fully than they had before the extent to which

Jesus was focused on the final state, or ultimate end of things. This 'eschatological' aspect of Jesus' teaching led them to appreciate a fundamental tension in his message. Sometimes he is clearly focused on how things will be at the end of time when there is a final judgement and everything will be decisively sorted out. On the other hand, there are aspects of what he says and how he says it that give the impression that this final horizon is not very far away at all, and is with us, though not fully, even now.

Certainly many of Jesus' early followers thought that the end was nigh. Our earliest forebears in the faith had a very limited sense of the future and it was only when time didn't abruptly end and the second coming didn't occur that subsequent generations began to rethink their faith – by now formalized somewhat into 'Christianity' – so that it might be sustainable over an extended period of time.

However, this delay in the coming or 'realization' of the kingdom of God does not detract in any degree from what Jesus has achieved through his mission to share our life, experience suffering and death, and triumph over evil at the resurrection. Any work that needed to be done to establish God's kingdom has been thoroughly and completely done, in, by and through Jesus Christ.

So the kingdom of God is established, but is also not yet here, though there might be intimations of it from time to time.

This is the tension in which Christian people now live, and which therefore shapes all our praying. The kingdom of God exists, but we are distant from it. We human beings cannot achieve it, but we seek it, hope for it, pray for it and on the negative side we can, by sin, frustrate its coming or fulfilment or manifestation. What the kingdom of God is not is a project or set of projects that we can achieve. We can think of it as God's project – as that on which God's attention, energy and determination is focused. And as such, God's kingdom and God's will are entirely aligned. What is not aligned with this superlative and complete divine effort is our own will – and that's why we have been taught to pray that God's kingdom will come and that God's will be done right here on earth.

9

THE PARABLE OF THE
DELAYED TRAIN

Imagine you are at a railway station waiting for a train to arrive. You know it has left London, but you don't know when it is due. For some reason, the train timetable you consulted yesterday is no longer accurate. The railway staff assure you that the train will definitely come, but no one knows when. Someone speculates that the problem is not with the train but with the signals 30 miles away. But no one is sure.

In a moment of quiet you pray that the train will arrive soon. It's a quiet prayer, but a vivid and sincere one, because it really matters to you that your journey continues. More than anything else you want to get off the draughty and cold platform and join the members of your family who are on the train already, and continue with them on the journey to visit your parents. It's not that anything is particularly time-critical. It's just that you know there will be fulfilment and the enjoyment of love when you get there that greatly surpasses the mutual alienation of the isolated individuals who are waiting for the same train on the windy platform.

Will your prayer make the train come any quicker? No. But you pray the prayer nonetheless as a way of focusing all your desire and energy on the hope for fulfilment that the train represents.

So you have prayed well.

And yet the train still doesn't arrive. Time ticks by. Slowly. You are concerned about your parents, who have been looking forward to this reunion for months and will now be getting worried. You wish you could communicate with them, but there is no way of getting a message through. You worry about your family members on the train, hoping that the lack of news doesn't mean that something awful has happened – a derailment, a collision at a level crossing, a terrorist attack even. You really should have charged your phone battery before you left rather than relying on being able to charge it once on the train.

You wait in self-contained silence and then someone standing by you strikes up a conversation. You are a bit irritated at first, as you were deriving some curmudgeonly pleasure from your sense of aggrieved frustration, but after a while the conversation is soothing and you begin to enjoy it. Someone else joins in and the conversation becomes more interesting. It's remarkable that you all have something in common in addition to the plan to travel north and the frustration of being on the platform. You look around the station and notice that all sorts of people who hadn't connected before are talking to each other.

When the train does arrive there is a great cheer, but the expected rush to seats is replaced by people exchanging phone numbers and shaking hands, and there are even a few hugs. Two former schoolfriends have been reunited after 50 years. You yourself meet a person who runs a campaigning organization that you will support in the future.

You find your family on the train and your sister tells you that she had in fact given your parents the wrong arrival date, so they won't be missing you in any case. The only problem will be that you are all going to arrive a day early. Someone has already called them and they are delighted.

KINGDOM – REALLY?

Any ancient religion that takes the written word seriously, that is any scriptural religion, needs to be sensitive to the meaning of words. This is why etymology is important in biblical scholarship and interpretation. It's really helpful to know where words have come from. But words have contemporary resonances that cannot be fathomed from their etymology. Some words are common in certain contexts but quite unusual and obscure in others. One person's jargon is another person's plain speech, and one person's poetic embellishment might be another person's worn-out metaphor or cliché.

In recent decades, feminist theologians have powerfully raised the question of the use of patriarchal language in the Bible and in theology. We have already had a brief consideration of this with regard to the word 'father'. The word 'kingdom' raises an overlapping set of issues.

The landmark Bible in English was the Authorized Version of 1611. That it was authorized tells us that an authority figure had endorsed it. That authority figure was none other than King James I of England (VI of Scotland), and King James was, obviously, a monarch.

It is neither necessary nor possible to spell out in detail here the extent to which Western ideas of kingship have informed the way in which we understand God. It is more important to note that reality – and also its opposite. For just as the reality of monarchy has informed the way we understand God, so the way in which we have understood God has informed the way in which the role and authority of earthly monarchs has been understood. As we identify these complementary dynamics, it is salutary to recall that when the Hebrew people first came up with the idea that it would be good to have a king, the prophet Samuel, the last of the judges, was extremely dubious about it. The enthusiasm of the people did very little to persuade him that this was a good idea and he was only prepared to accept the plan because he believed that God had assured him that the people should have their way in this regard. In a famous speech Samuel warned them what to expect if they were to vest power and authority in one individual, anticipating the dictum of the nineteenth-century Lord Acton that 'power tends to corrupt and absolute power corrupts absolutely'.

> [The king] will appoint for himself commanders of thousands and commanders of fifties, and some to plough his ground and to reap his harvest, and to make his implements of war and the equipment of his chariots. He will take your daughters to be perfumers and cooks and bakers. He will take the best of your fields and vineyards and olive orchards and give them to his courtiers. He will take one-tenth of your grain and of your vineyards and give it to his officers and his courtiers. He will take your male and female slaves, and the best of your cattle and donkeys, and put them to his work. He will take one-tenth of your flocks, and you shall be his slaves. And in that day you will cry out because of your king, whom you have chosen for yourselves; but the LORD will not answer you in that day. (1 Samuel 8.12-18)

When Jesus spoke of the 'kingdom' of God, he was not, of course, intending to invoke a social and political order dominated by the self-serving use of power by the powerful. There is no suggestion in the phrase that he meant to imply human hierarchy in which the few had power to control the many and thereby serve their own ends. Nor is there any hint that by using the phrase he intended to condone the aggregation of personal wealth and privilege by those who had acquired or were given political power.

In other words, when Jesus spoke of the kingdom of God, the emphasis was not on kingdom but on God. The word 'kingdom' is intended to signify some sort of secure ordering of society and relationships, but what the words 'of God' add to it is vital. The kingdom of God is the ordering of relationships and society in accord with the nature, influence and power of God. Such a kingdom will obviously be very different to any kingdom that is ordered by human desire to control or self-interest. It will be different too from any society ordered by well-meaning but misguided idealism. It is life lived under the law of grace.

The emphasis in this phrase is not, therefore, on the kingly aspect of kingdom, but on the divine, and therefore the graceful – grace-filled – aspect. The negative aspects of what power does to the powerful, and the impact of this on their societies, is precisely what the phrase 'kingdom *of God*' is intended to subvert. The literal translation we considered in Chapter 1 makes it clear: 'let come the kingdom of you' – not the kingdom of anyone else. If we allowed ourselves a few more words, we might paraphrase this as: 'let our social and political order reflect God's loving-kindness and justice – not human fear and greed'.

THE KIN-DOM OF GOD

For some people, perhaps a growing number of people, the word 'kingdom' will never be rid of its unhelpful connotations. The word has accumulated just too much baggage over too long a period to be useful in prayer, and, worse perhaps, is understood to be giving quite the wrong message to those who are seeking to understand the faith that they are tentatively making their own. The issue here is not fundamentally different to the problem with the word 'father', but it is somewhat more deeply embedded, as there is no parallel phrase that we can use here to match 'motherly father'.

A subtle and helpful suggestion has been made, however, which, while almost a pun, can help people today get more of a feel for what Jesus had in mind when he spoke about a divine 'kingdom'. The idea was given prominence in the writing of the late Dr Ada María Isasi-Díaz in her book, *Mujerista Theology*.

It is simple enough. Rather than pray for the coming of God's kingdom, we should pray for the coming of God's kin-dom.

Removing the 'g' doesn't make a huge difference to the way the word sounds, but it has a huge impact on how we understand it. Whereas the word 'kingdom' suggests a vertical hierarchy, kin-dom suggests a horizontal solidarity. In fact, it is in the context of emphasizing the importance of true solidarity that Isasi-Díaz introduces the 'kin-dom' idea. She writes from the perspective of Hispanic or Latina women who live in the United States, the mujerista. These women are only too aware of the extent to which their lives are limited and controlled by sexism, racism and economic oppression. Her intention is to give priority to solidarity over the notion of charity, which she sees as too one-sided to reflect Christian ideals. But she is also aware that 'solidarity' is a concept that has been corrupted and cheapened.

For Isasi-Díaz, solidarity is not a feeling of connection, nor is it a matter of agreement with a group taking a certain position. True solidarity is the union of 'kindred persons' who have a common interest and whose relationships are imbued with mutuality. Solidarity is the virtue of those who accept their interconnectedness and then respond to the oppression, pain and injustice experienced by others as if they were members of the same caring family.

Dropping the 'g' from 'kingdom' offers a challenge to move not only from charity to solidarity but also from complacency to concern and engagement. It is to move away from the perspective that thinks, with nineteenth-century poet, Robert Browning, 'God's in his heaven——/ All's right with the world' to the perspective of the mujerista living in the United States, who experience the underside of oppressive structures quite personally, and who know that charitable handouts will never lead to justice for them or their families.

One of the more constructive social responses to the early phases of the impact of Covid-19 on our communities was the recognition that key workers include many in low-paid jobs, and, in particular, that the work of caring for others – that is, meeting the basic bodily and practical basic needs of the vulnerable – is poorly paid and hugely undervalued in Western societies. People who say the Lord's Prayer regularly might expect to feel increasingly uncomfortable that those whose work is vital to the wellbeing of others and the functioning of society are under-rewarded for their efforts.

The irony here, of course, is that those who really do exercise care for others are, in fact, behaving in a way that reflects the 'kin-ship' that is the ideal and goal of our prayer. In terms of Christian values, they are high achievers. The hoped-for result of the prayer might therefore be that we come to see and value care not as something to be attended to when the more important things on our to-do list have been ticked off, but as something quite fundamental to who we are, and intrinsic to God's intentions for the wellbeing and fulfilment of us all.

12

WHAT THE PRAYER IS NOT

We have come to the point where it is completely clear that the Lord's Prayer is not, perhaps, the bland source of assurance that we sometimes want or need it to be. Not only is it like a poem, full of meaning and open to fresh interpretation; it is also full of ethical as well as spiritual challenge. Although we pray it daily and when we are especially lost for words, we realize now that it might not always speak to the somewhat sorry state of mind and heart in which we find ourselves. The Lord's Prayer is not always a ready source of comfort, even though a desire for warm affirmation can sometimes feel like our most pressing spiritual need.

What, then, might be a prayer that reflects our spiritual starting point as modern people? Something like this, perhaps:

Dear God, my own special God in my own heart,
let me have peace of mind,

fulfil all my desires,

and take away all my guilt and shame.

Lead me not into suffering,

keep me free of pain,

and deliver me from tribulation and despair,

for then I will be happy, safe and secure;

and you will become worthy of my praise.

There are probably aspects of this formulation that we can all relate to. Who does not crave peace of mind? What are personal desires if we do not wish them to be fulfilled? Who does not long for their guilt and shame to be taken away 'just like that' with no questions asked or no obligations taken on? And none of us want to be subject to suffering, pain, tribulation or despair, so why should we not pray for such deliverance?

The prayer, however, is most unlike prayer as taught by Jesus. The give-away is in its self-regard. The 'God' who is being prayed to here is 'my own special God'; that's bad enough, but the worst part of the prayer is that the end-point reveals that the intention of the prayer, as far as the praying person is concerned, is for God to take the opportunity to prove that God is praise-worthy in our sight. Such sentiments are found in the book of Psalms, but they are a very long way indeed from the spirit of the prayer that Jesus taught us.

This may come as something of a shock, but the Lord's Prayer is not a prayer for personal happiness, safety and security. Such concepts are quite alien to it, though, as we will see, there are words in the prayer that allow us to bring our basic needs to God. They do so, however, in such a way as to meet those needs, not to satisfy our desires for a happy and contented life on our own terms. Indeed, it is not too much to suggest that the Lord's Prayer is an invitation to take Jesus' perspective to heart so thoroughly that we find ourselves living life on his terms and not our own.

The prayer that I have written here is an entirely understandable prayer to most people today. Some may have grown out of sentiments like this, but for many of us there is a part of who we are that wants to pray, and maybe still does pray, in just those sorts of terms. And we should be honest about it. It is not a prayer in the spirit of Jesus so much as a prayer in the spirit of ego; it is, to put it bluntly, the prayer of a narcissist. That does not make it a dishonest or bad prayer. Indeed, there is a very strong argument that if this is what you feel then this is what you should pray.

Prayer should always be a matter of integrity, not of performance or hypocrisy.

Honesty is more important in prayer than correctness, but it is important also to realize, even when we whisper, speak or maybe shout out our heartfelt desires and our anxiety-filled prayers for protection, that the likely outcome of such an activity is not going to be some change in God's mind or will, but some sort of transformation of us. When we pray prayers like this, we are not twisting God's arm, however cleverly manipulative we think we are being – 'you do this God, and I'll reward you with praise'. No, what we are doing is exposing ourselves, in all our spiritual vulnerability, to the motherly Father who will understand and accept us, offering us the unconditional love that will begin to take us towards maturity; not as a quid pro quo, but as a relational response. All thought of calculated exchange is inappropriate here. It's more like the way in which we smile back at someone who smiles at us. Praise of God is not like the praise of a schoolchild. It is the unaffected affirmation of a reality that calls from us more delight than we can contain.

The prayer that Jesus taught is radically different to the prayer of a contemporary narcissist, because it is the prayer of a humble disciple. Such a person focuses first on the love and holiness of God. Second, they accept that relating to God means relating kindly and lovingly towards all other people. Third, as we shall see more clearly as we progress, they will focus on their own material and spiritual needs – 'bread' and 'forgiveness'. They will then appreciate that there is never any cause for complacency, because temptation and evil are always close at hand. Such a person finally returns with confidence and delight to the assurance that the power and glory belong to the holy One who is indeed the motherly father of us all.

That's the Lord's Prayer in a nutshell. Our challenge is to make it our own.

PART THREE

BREAD

Give us this day our daily bread.

There is no competition between the vertical concerns of God and the horizontal concerns of humanity. Both meet under the rainbow of prayer.

Leonardo Boff

13

BREAD AND WISDOM

Anyone who is reasonably familiar with Christianity will appreciate that it is a religion that cares about bread. Whether we think of the well-loved Welsh hymn with its rousing chorus, 'Bread of heaven, bread of heaven, feed me till I want no more', or of the service of Holy Communion where bread is taken, blessed, broken and shared as the body of Christ, it is clear that bread matters. For a Christian, the word 'bread' carries more than material significance. Yes, bread is bread, but it can also be more than bread. And for that reason, this is a richer and more complicated part of the prayer than we might at first realize.

Although bread is often taken to represent the most basic form of nutrition, even ordinary bread is a more complex and diverse reality than we normally recognize. 'Bread and water' are punishment rations, but go to a supermarket today and you will be overwhelmed by the variety of both. We desire and need simplicity in our prayer, and what could be simpler than 'bread'? But as soon as you begin to reflect on 'bread', you realize that even basic nourishment comes in diverse forms. Not only are there different shapes and sizes of loaf, but there are also many different flours that can be used; these in turn might be milled to different extents and blended in different proportions. There are different leavening agents too; and in any case, not all bread is leavened, nor is all bread baked – the world of flat breads offers another realm of variety altogether.

If our prayer for daily bread is meant to symbolize our reliance on God for our basic sustenance day by day, then it would seem that the modern world has done much to obscure and complicate matters. Nevertheless, it might be that the variety we have now come to associate with bread is actually quite a helpful way to understand this part of the prayer – since as human beings even our most basic bodily needs are quite diverse and complex. But important as material needs are, there is more to us than the body, and, as Jesus reminded the devil when he was tempted to conjure up some food to eat from stones in the desert, 'One does not live by bread alone' (Matthew 4.4). The meaning of 'bread' is narrow here, but the meaning of bread in the Lord's Prayer is much more expansive. Not 'bread' as in 'bread and water', but 'bread' as in the wonderful variety that we know today.

But there is more to bread than even this. When Jesus answered the devil, he continued his quote by saying, 'but by every word that proceeds from the mouth of God'. The meaning of bread in the Lord's Prayer does not extend as far as being a metaphor for God's word, but there is a strong and deep tradition of seeing in it the most sacred of meanings. So the bread here has been taken to refer not only to a variety of material needs but also to the whole range of needs that human beings experience.

In a remarkable little book that meditates on the Aramaic text of the Lord's Prayer, Neil Douglas-Klotz says that the Aramaic word that Jesus would have used had the meaning of both 'bread' and 'understanding', which he sees as 'food for all forms of growth and for elementary life in general'. He connects this understanding with the feminine personification of 'holy wisdom' mentioned in the book of Proverbs. This is not an approach that has been taken up by many Christian theologians, but it is notable that Thomas Aquinas himself taught that the word 'bread' could have two meanings: 'bodily bread' and 'the bread of wisdom'.

The sense in Aquinas seems to be that the bread petition is fundamentally our opportunity to ask for whatever we need in order not only to survive but also to fulfil our obligations and to live out our vocation. Preaching on this petition in Naples, he shared what was perhaps a rather personal reflection. 'It often happens that a person of great learning and wisdom becomes fearful and timid, and needs, as a result, fortitude of heart lest he lack necessities.' Fortitude, or courage, and understanding, or wisdom, are complementary gifts and virtues without which it is impossible to imagine a human being achieving anything great, or even worthy. While it might seem to be a stretch of the word 'bread' to include the request for such inner strengths, if we do not allow them into our prayer under the heading of 'bread' it is difficult to see how they will enter. The key word here is 'necessities' – and the petition for bread concerns both our need of them and our anxieties about how we might manage if they are not available.

BREAD AND JUSTICE

One of the most powerful presentations on the meaning of this petition was given in the fourth century by Gregory of Nyssa. Like his older brother Basil, by whom he was educated, Gregory was a very significant thinker and bishop at a time when the Church was formulating its core doctrines. In his sermons on the Lord's Prayer, he is less concerned to make subtle points as to be fundamentally clear about basic meanings. For Gregory, the prayer for bread in the Lord's Prayer is significant precisely because of its modesty. When we pray it, we are seeking 'only what is sufficient to preserve our physical existence'.

So we say to God: Give us bread. Not delicacies or riches, nor magnificent purple robes, golden ornaments, precious stones, or silver dishes. Nor do we ask Him for landed estates, or military commands, or political leadership. We pray neither for herds of horses and oxen or other cattle in great numbers, nor for a host of slaves. We do not say, give us a prominent position in assemblies or monuments and statues raised to us, nor silken robes and musicians at meals, nor any other thing by which the soul is estranged from the thought of God and higher things; no – but only bread!

We can imagine Gregory surveying the way in which members of the Church, like others, preoccupied themselves with the pursuit of luxuries and pleasures that in his view added nothing of value to life at all. For Gregory the pursuit of 'vanities' only has the effect of creating more work. The rhetoric of his argument is energetic and powerful. The point is to content yourself with what is necessary. Everything else takes more from you than it delivers – he calls it 'tribute' and refers to the stomach as 'this perpetual tax collector'. The thought of Gregory in a well-stocked supermarket or surveying the latest range of cookery books or watching television programmes devoted to celebrating the gourmet arts is a troubling one. He would not be impressed at all, and would seek to put all this astonishing stuff into perspective. To return to his sermon:

... the loveliness of sight or smell or taste presents the senses with very transitory delight; except for the palate, there is no difference in the foods consumed, for nature changes all things equally into an evil smell. Do you see the end of fine cookery? Do you realize the result of wizard flavourings? Ask for bread because life needs it, and you owe it to the body because of your nature.

Appreciating that this emphasis on seeking no more than a subsistence diet might not be greeted with enthusiasm by those who enjoy the pleasures of the table, Gregory proposes a reliance on the 'flavouring that is provided by nature itself'. He is not proposing that we should wander into the garden to pick some basil or thyme, still less hunt out exotic spices on market stalls.

[Nature's flavouring] is above all a good conscience which makes the bread tasty because it is eaten in justice. But if you want to enjoy also the physical sense of taste, let hunger be your flavouring; do not overeat yourself so that you have no appetite because you are feeling sick. But let the sweat mentioned in the commandment precede your meal – *In sweat and labour shalt thou eat thy bread*. You see this is the first kind of flavour scripture mentions.

If the Fair Trade movement has yet to adopt a patron saint, it might be that Gregory of Nyssa is their person. His concern is certainly with the way in which our appetite for food can distract and corrupt us; but his eye also rests on the social and political consequences of greed. As his sermon continues, the focus on justice becomes more intense. Justice is not a 'nice to have', but something of the most fundamental, one might say sacred, importance.

Gregory has insisted on the ordinariness of the bread for which we pray in the Lord's Prayer, but he has not taken us away from God. Rather he has drawn us closer to God by placing God's values and priorities squarely before us and showing how they are connected to our ordinary living, even our 'daily bread'.

Give Thou bread – that is to say, let me have food through just labour. For if God is justice, the man who procures himself food through covetousness cannot have his bread from God. You are the master of your prayer, if abundance does not come from another's property and is not the result of another's tears; if no one is hungry or distressed because you are fully satisfied. For the bread of God is above all the fruit of justice, the ear of the corn of peace, pure and without any admixture of the seed of tares.

Gregory speaks to us prophetically from fourth-century Nyssa. Food, he tells us, is a spiritual issue. But as well as the whole question of eating and what we allow our appetites to do to our souls, there are questions that lie behind the reality of who ends up with what on their plate and in their stomach. For Gregory there is a direct line from these words of the Lord's Prayer to the highest and most pressing demand of God: justice.

15

DAILY BREAD

One of the major influences on Gregory of Nyssa was also one of the earliest commentators on the Lord's Prayer. This Greek-speaking thinker called Origen, who lived in Alexandria in the late third and early fourth centuries, was the first to draw attention to something very odd about the adjective that we now translate as 'daily'. He noticed that the Greek word in question, *epiousios*, is super-rare. Seeking to find it somewhere else in the Gospels – he failed. Looking across the whole New Testament – he couldn't see it. Scouring the whole of known Greek literature – the search was equally fruitless.

So what is the story of *epiousios*, the only adjective in the prayer? It is almost always translated 'daily', but is that really what it means? This matters because adjectives qualify the meaning of nouns. Suppose that *epiousios* didn't mean daily as in everyday or ordinary, but something quite different – 'special' for instance, or maybe 'spiritual'. If this was the case then the petition would have a very different meaning.

This book is meant to be an immersion in the Lord's Prayer and at this point that means we must peer into the deep historical well that is the story of the way in which the word *epiousios* has been translated and understood.

Having noted that Origen was perplexed by the word in the third century, we move on to the fourth century and consider the contribution of Jerome, who, as it happens, was a near contemporary of our friend Gregory of Nyssa. Jerome's great work was to create a new Latin version of the Bible, which became known as the Vulgate, based on Hebrew texts of the Old Testament and Greek texts of the New Testament. Intriguingly, Jerome translated the word *epiousios* differently in the Gospels of Matthew and Luke. In Matthew he used the literal *super-substantialem* or 'super-substantial', but in Luke he used *quotidianum*, which has quite different resonances, meaning 'ordinary' or 'everyday'. In choosing these two different words he framed the two ways in which the word 'bread' has been understood in this context down the centuries. There are those who have seen it as bread that is super-substantial, meaning 'more than material' or, as we might now say, 'spiritual'. To others it is quite the opposite: it is ordinary, mundane or 'staple'; not the fancy food of a feast or party but the nourishment that we need day by day. It is this second meaning that eventually won out in the Roman Church and if you listen to the Lord's Prayer being said or sung in Latin today it is the word *quotidianum* that you will hear.

The story of the translation of *epiousios* in English, which was often by way of Latin, is also intriguing. An Anglo-Saxon version of the prayer uses two words here: *ofer wistlic*. *Wistlic* means 'provision' or 'substance' and *ofer* means 'more'. The sense seems to be that we are asking for something more than bodily provisions. This sense is also found in the fourteenth-century translation of the Bible by John Wycliffe: 'geue to us this day oure breed ouir other substaunce'. In 'other substaunce' we hear a clear echo of super-substantial.

It is in William Tyndale's early sixteenth-century version of the Bible that we first get the word 'daily' as the translation of *epiousios*. And there it has remained ever since, carrying with it the sense of everyday or ordinary, and having now lost all sense of 'super-substantial' or 'spiritual'.

This development towards the ordinary and away from the spiritual can also be seen in the work of Martin Luther. In his earlier writings, Luther took the approach that the bread for which we are invited to pray was not material and bodily but spiritual, reflecting the 'super-substantial' interpretation. In his later writing, he was far more down to earth in his interpretation of what the petition might mean. While there were sound theological reasons for Luther to change his mind, there were also historic and practical factors. In particular, the crop failures in Europe in the 1520s and the hardships created by the Peasants' War of 1525 stand between his two interpretations. It would be a very other-worldly pastor who would insist that the Lord commanded us only to ask for the bread of heaven when surrounded by people whose prayers for daily bread came from hearts resting heavily on their empty stomachs.

Calvin, writing in the following decade, was more trenchant. 'What certain writers say in philosophizing about "supersubstantial bread" seems to me to agree very little with Christ's meaning; indeed, if we did not even in this fleeting life accord to God the office of nourisher, this would be an imperfect prayer.'

The consensus is broadly along the lines that the bread for which we pray is the ordinary everyday stuff that we need to keep body and soul together. Translators and users of the prayer seem to be happy with the word 'daily', though there are some who have entered into a discussion about whether the word is better thought of as meaning 'of this day' or 'of tomorrow'. Indeed, if we peer even further into the well of this word, we find suggestions such as 'for the end time' or 'that comes to us from the future', and some believe that the overall meaning here is 'bread for the journey'.

This can all be rather confusing – not least because there is another reference to time in the same sentence: the phrase translated 'this day'.

We can comfortably conclude, however, that the adjective that qualifies bread in the Lord's Prayer does not mean that we should only pray for bread that is special or spiritual. It is everyday material nourishment that is in focus here, the adjective serving to emphasize the ordinariness of what we seek and thereby underlining the point that God's concern and engagement is with us as bodily beings who have basic needs, and therefore fundamental worries about our survival. As we shall see, however, although the adjective does not mean that we are praying for 'spiritual bread', there is more to the bread that we seek than 'bread alone'.

I 6

DAY BY DAY

We have given more than enough attention to the adjective 'daily', but have yet to focus on the words 'this day' that are also an important part of this petition.

'Give us *this day* our daily bread.' The most obvious question to ask about this petition is why it refers only to this day – or 'today' as modern versions render it.

Thinking back to all the fairy stories in which someone is granted three wishes, we recollect that the invitation to make a wish is an opportunity to express practical wisdom and prudence. If this prayer is in effect a wish for food, might it not be smarter to pray for food every day than just for today. Not, 'Give us *this* day our daily bread', but, 'Give us *each* day our daily bread'? In fact, this is precisely what Luke has in his version.

This is an area that hasn't been as extensively over-thought by scholars as the 'daily' question, but there is a connection that we can make with an area of contemporary and historic concern that makes this an especially fascinating, deep and important question. The question is: what do we mean by the present moment?

Focus on this subject is something that we perhaps associate more with Buddhism than with Christianity. The practice of mindfulness, and its cousin meditation, are far subtler and more sophisticated than they might first seem, but one aspect of them is the attempt to draw our consciousness away from the habits of relentless and anxious speculation about the future, or repetitive rumination about the past. The refuge from these comes in the present moment, the episode of time that we inhabit right now. In mindfulness, the means to this existential engagement is to be found in paying attention, as much attention as possible, to basic material sensations, whether it is sights or sounds or what we can touch or smell. We notice that which we generally ignore while distracted by mental chatter, and thereby quieten our minds.

Meditation, on the other hand, often begins with attention directed inwards, to the breath that we draw into our bodies and then exhale again. Breathing is controlled and comes into focus so that, in meditation, we can forget ourselves and anticipate, perhaps, that selflessness that is at once liberation and fulfilment.

These matters are much more easily said than done, as many (perhaps all) who have tried them will have discovered early on. One thing that we often fail to take into account when engaging in such practices is that you cannot observe or admire your own self-forgetfulness. As soon as you say, 'Oh, good for me, I'm now meditating; I'm thinking about nothing, in fact I'm really blissed out with the lack of anxiety', you have blown it because you are now full of thought – about your meditating self. Such self-admiration is not the absence of self of which the Buddhists speak and it is clearly not an act of self-giving, which is at the top of the list of Christian values. It is self-focus. Peaceful and non-anxious self-focus perhaps, and in that regard it is much better than the way we spend a lot of our time, but it is still not the real deal of self-forgetfulness.

Christianity and Buddhism both value self-forgetfulness, but among the factors that inform the way they approach this are their conceptions of time. In particular, their conceptions of the present moment are not identical. Christianity, like Judaism, tends to see things in historical terms – one thing leading to another and everything progressing or at least changing over time. For Christians, time is chronological. Life has direction, and history is moving towards an end not only in the sense of a 'terminus' but also in the sense that it has a 'purpose'. Certainly Christianity is aware of moments of significance and times of opportunity; the New Testament uses the Greek work *kairos* in addition to the word *chronos*, which refers to linear time. *Kairos* matters in Christianity, and various 'kairos documents' have been produced in recent decades; for example, the South African Kairos Document of 1985 and the Kairos Palestine document of 2009, both of which analysed a situation of injustice and quite rightly urged on their readers the importance of action and a new beginning. It is not to diminish the importance of *kairos* or kairos documents to make the point that such moments of opportunity sit in chronological time. A *kairos* is not an opportunity to step out of the flow of *chronos*, but to make a significant, history-changing, intervention. *Kairos* matters not because of today but because of all the tomorrows that can be shaped by decisive action now.

This is not, however, how Buddhism relates to the moment. If you ask a Christian monk to show you their watch, it will be very much like your own. If you ask a Zen or Chan Buddhist the same question, they may well show you an analogue dial that doesn't have the numerals 3, 6, 9 and 12 at the quarter points but instead has the words 'now', 'now', 'now' and 'now'. The Buddhist moment is time out of time. It is now, on repeat.

The reference to 'this day' or 'today' in the Lord's Prayer cannot be equated with a Buddhist sense of the present moment as 'now on repeat', as that wrist-watch suggests, because in Christianity 'the present always impinges on the future' – which is why a *kairos* moment can be so important. Nonetheless, while not in quite the same territory as the Buddhist emphasis on the present moment, 'the day' does have the similarity that it is a time of limited (though admittedly much longer) duration and enriched significance. In this regard we are all like Shakespeare's Macbeth: when we think of the future, it is 'tomorrow and tomorrow and tomorrow', and when we think of the past, it is 'all our yesterdays'. But when we think of the present tense, when we think of now, we need not think only of the micro-moment between the drawing in and expelling of our breath, or that tiny gap between the two beats of our heart, but also of the 24-hour period of light and darkness that makes our day.

The Jews have the week with its Sabbath, but Jesus was not by any means an enthusiast for the Sabbath; nor, it seems, was Paul. Jesus saw it as a means to an end, famously saying that 'The sabbath was made for humankind, and not humankind for the sabbath' when he was challenged for breaking it (Mark 2.27). Paul saw it as of no greater significance than festivals or new moons, writing that all these were 'only a shadow of what is to come' (Colossians 2.17). And both neglected to mention it when they summarized the Ten Commandments (see Mark 10.19 and Romans 13.9). The Buddhists, as we have seen, have their present moment, but for the Christian it is perhaps the 'day' that matters most. Jesus put this negatively when he said, 'So do not worry about tomorrow, for tomorrow will bring worries of its own. Today's trouble is enough for today' (Matthew 6.34). But maybe he was also implying the opposite: 'today's blessing is enough for today'. When it comes to the prayer for provisions, the prayer for bread, one meaning that we should perhaps live with and seek to make our own in prayer is simply: 'Give us enough for now', that is, for 'today'.

A question remains, however, and it can be put like this. What happens after now? What about tomorrow? My suggestion is that when we pray for daily bread now, we are not being entirely negligent about the future, but that preparation for the future is part of what needs to happen in every now that we ever live through. Every day is the beginning of the rest of your life, as the cliché has it, and as we have already noted, a *kairos* moment gains its significance primarily because of its power to create consequences. This might be to move a little from the radical limits of concern expressed in Matthew's version of the prayer, which doesn't seem to have much thought to the future, but it is entirely consistent with Luke's version 'Give us each day'. The Christian attitude towards the future is not denial that it is coming, but a stance of anticipatory stewardship towards it. We pray for our bread today so that we may care positively for tomorrow.

17

BREAD, AND YET
MORE THAN BREAD

We have already noted that Martin Luther changed his mind about the meaning of the bread petition, moving away from a spiritual to a bodily interpretation. In his *Small Catechism* of 1529, he embraces this new way of understanding it and draws up an extensive list to explain its range of meaning. He lists: 'food, drink, clothes, shoes, houses, farms, fields, lands, money, property, a good marriage, good children, honest and faithful public servants, a just government, favourable weather (neither too hot nor too cold!), health, honours, good friends, loyal neighbours'.

As Karl Barth comments, when writing about this in the mid-twentieth century, this list neatly identified the needs of the farming bourgeoisie of sixteenth-century Germany. Luther is quite right to expand the meaning of bread to include all that is needed. As Barth comments, 'nothing hinders us from interpreting and expanding it according to the needs of our time and of our individual situations'. Gregory of Nyssa might not have been quite so sympathetic, seeing here perhaps some rather extravagant 'wants' among the 'needs'. For Barth, though, the list is somewhat overpowering and so he seeks to recapture what he calls the *simplicity* of the original word 'bread'.

Given what we have already discovered about bread, we might doubt that he is going to find that things are completely simple. And we would be right. For Barth, the Bible, always for him the most important point of reference, offers two distinct meanings of bread. First, it refers to the basics needed to subsist in this life. The bread that answers for this necessity *today* also brings with it the question of tomorrow. To address this, Barth remains in the Bible, reminding us that God's people have always been a wilderness people who, when they complained that they were at risk of starvation, were given the gift of manna to sustain them.

The story of manna is told in the sixteenth chapter of the book of Exodus. The manna is described as bread but also rather puzzlingly likened to 'coriander seed'. Apparently, it tasted 'like wafers made with honey'. The image that springs to my mind is the breakfast cereal that is now called Honey Monster Wheat Puffs but which I remember from my childhood as Sugar Puffs (an extravagance only rarely allowed, as I recall). The significant point about manna, however, was not the taste or size, but the use-by date. The manna that God provided only lasted for one day, except that on the eve of the Sabbath a more durable manna was provided, so that the Sabbath needs could be met without labour. The point was clear. Focus on the moment; the day. Trust that the God who provides for today will also provide for tomorrow. Your role in this is not to plan or to store but to trust.

This same approach permeated Jesus' teaching. In Matthew's Sermon on the Mount he warns against storing up treasure on earth, but encourages people to have their treasure in heaven (Matthew 6.19-21) and in Luke we find the Parable of the Rich Fool:

'The land of a rich man produced abundantly. And he thought to himself, "What should I do, for I have no place to store my crops?" Then he said, "I will do this: I will pull down my barns and build larger ones, and there I will store all my grain and my goods. And I will say to my soul, Soul, you have ample goods laid up for many years; relax, eat, drink, be merry." But God said to him, "You fool! This very night your life is being demanded of you. And the things you have prepared, whose will they be?" So it is with those who store up treasures for themselves but are not rich towards God.' (Luke 12.16-21)

You could say that Jesus encourages us to have, not a hoarding-mentality, but a manna-mentality.

Barth's second meaning of 'bread' is that it is also 'the temporal sign of God's eternal grace'. For him bread is at once presence and promise. 'Bread is the mysterious presence of this food which, after it has been eaten, does not need to be replaced.' The most powerful biblical reference here is to be found in the sixth chapter of John's Gospel where, when faced with a challenge to his authority, Jesus refers to himself as the 'living bread'.

'Our ancestors ate the manna in the wilderness; as it is written, "He gave them bread from heaven to eat."' Then Jesus said to them, 'Very truly, I tell you, it was not Moses who gave you the bread from heaven, but it is my Father who gives you the true bread from heaven. For the bread of God is that which comes down from heaven and gives life to the world.' They said to him, 'Sir, give us this bread always.'

Jesus said to them, 'I am the bread of life. Whoever comes to me will never be hungry, and whoever believes in me will never be thirsty.' (John 6.31-35)

Once again, focus on the spiritual serves not as a retreat to the ethereal but as a gateway to earthy realism. Like Gregory of Nyssa, Karl Barth finds a strong connection with justice wrapped up with the bread of the Lord's Prayer. 'How shameful is our social ingratitude and injustice!' he writes. 'How senseless it is that in this humanity surrounded by thy gifts there are people still dying of hunger!'

For Karl Barth, meditation on bread, with its two parallel sets of meanings, brings us to the highest possible level of significance and purpose: to the level of grace itself. Vitally, this is not at the expense of the everyday, nor does it involve neglecting consideration of our material needs. 'Reality' and 'sign' are not alternatives for Barth; they are fully and vitally integrated. Bread addresses hunger, but it leads not just to fullness of the belly but to fullness of life. 'One shall not live by bread alone', certainly, but the bread that God gives is both bread and more than bread.

For Barth, the unadorned petition for bread means:

> Give us this minimum which is necessary for the present moment; and at the same time, give it to us as a sign, as a pledge anticipating our whole life. According to thy promise, which we are receiving at this moment, we receive also the presence of thine eternal goodness, the assurance that we shall live with thee.

It's a little opaque, perhaps, but if you think that bread is like love, it begins to become clear. No one can give you love for the future. It is as our relationships develop that we get a feel for whether or not the person who loves us today is also promising love for the future. However, you really do have to trust them for it. There can be no gift that is my love for next week or next year or for ten or thirty years' time. And so it is with God and bread. What we gratefully receive today we anticipate hopefully for tomorrow. As we pray for bread and receive it, so we grow not only in our desire for justice but also in faith and hope.

18

MANNA-MENTALITY AND THE FOODIE GENERATION

It is now abundantly clear that the short petition for daily bread in the Lord's Prayer is not as simple or as straightforward as we might first have thought. It might sound like we are placing an order with a baker, but while there is an element of basic request here, there is also something far subtler and more important going on. When we pray this petition, we are putting our basic bodily needs before God, but we are doing so in a particular way and in a certain context. The effect is to align us with God's agenda for justice and to invite us to live by trust in God. Yes, the petition is fundamentally about basic bodily needs and vulnerabilities, but its symbolic meaning also taps into our deepest desires and most enduring hopes.

Much of this might be obscure to people today, not because they lack vulnerability or hope but because their life has become so cluttered and complicated.

We have already had to acknowledge that for us there is no such single simple thing as bread – we live in a world of many breads. But that's just the tip of the iceberg of the complexity of our relationship with food today. We enjoy our food, but what can we say about the spiritualty of our eating?

Many of us live with more cookery books than prayer books in our homes, and we spend more money and emotion on the wonderful world of food than any previous generation. The exposure to food in supermarkets, cafes and restaurants, and through glamourous advertising, is something that we have come to take as part of the wallpaper of life, forgetting how historically and culturally unusual it is to be presented with nothing short of abundance all the time.

The negative side of this abundance is obvious, but complicated, with issues as diverse as eating disorders, obesity, intensive agriculture and waste, not to mention inequality of access to food, leading to the proliferation of food banks and soup kitchens in recent years. All of these contemporary realities are connected by an approach to food that is distant to the sort of relationship to it that the Lord's Prayer might encourage.

Where, then, does that leave the conscientious pray-er of this prayer? In practical terms we might ask whether our recitation of the Lord's Prayer has ever impacted on our own shopping habits or indeed on our storage habits. We might even ask whether the Parable of the Rich Fool is one that has a special relevance for us today.

And what about panic-buying? Surely regular exposure to the Lord's Prayer would disincline us from such an activity, reinforcing in us the manna-mentality that Jesus commended. Indeed, a strict and literal reading of Jesus' teaching would seem to rule out not only panic-buying but all forms of storage: domestic fridges and freezers and the use of artificial preservatives are suddenly rendered suspect. Canned foods, pickles and jams, not to mention the salted and dried provisions that kept our grandparents going, could be seen as sources of guilt and shame. Is this really what the gospel requires of us and our larders? Does a manna-mentality demand a return to day-to-day subsistence?

That seems to me an imprudent and wasteful proposition – a perverse refusal to accept the positive aspects of cultural and scientific advance. We need to embrace a concept of anticipatory stewardship.

And on a more basic level, surely a family facing the prospect of being asked to quarantine or self-isolate would be well advised to have an adequately stocked larder and freezer.

What the gospel requires of us, rather, is a grateful, proportionate (or just) and non-anxious relationship not only with food but with all the provisions we need in order to live a good life. We need to nourish ourselves and contribute to the needs of others. The point is to recognize that whatever we have, however much we have earned it, remains in some sense a gift. As John Calvin wrote when commenting on this petition: 'what is in our hand is not even ours except in so far as he bestows each little portion upon us hour by hour, and allows us to use it'.

As human beings we know we are fearful in the face of deprivation, but as those who pray the Lord's Prayer we know that a right relationship with God is developed when we seek to have our own needs met while not neglecting the need for justice for all. To do this we need to have faith in God's provision to the extent that trust replaces the anxiety that drives us to behave in ways that are bad for us and bad for others. At the same time, we must avoid the path of

Luddite irresponsibility that would prevent us making adequate provision for the future.

Perhaps even more fundamentally than this, it's important to recognize that we pray not as people who have got ourselves sorted out and who are on top of our own negativity, always able to do the right things for the right reasons all the time. We pray as those who need to pray; as those who know their need of God. Prayer isn't reserved for those who have *overcome* their fear and anxiety, but is for those who know that unless they reach out for spiritual support they will be even more vulnerable to fear and anxiety – leading on perhaps to panic – becoming the main drivers of their actions.

Someone who prays the Lord's Prayer might find themselves panic-buying, or one day see their store cupboards in a new light and realize that they really have been hoarding. They might even take a look at their finances and realize that, despite the financial fears they have been living with for years, they are, it seems, quite well-off. The difference between the praying panic-buyer or hoarder, or the person who has accumulated more money than they expected, and those who do not pray as Jesus taught us is that the one who prays might be brought up short by their prayer and begin to feel the tension between purporting to live by faith and prayer, when their actions have in fact been driven by anxiety and have led to unnecessary accumulation.

Quite how to respond to that tension is a real pastoral issue. It should not be addressed negatively – 'What you have done is terrible' – but positively – 'Now that you understand the situation more fully you can make some better choices.' Christian spirituality is very positive about the future; it is a religion of hope. We may have got things wrong in the past, but the future gives us scope to put them right. That's why the future is so important. It means that we are not trapped by the past or locked into the present.

PART FOUR

FORGIVENESS

And forgive us our trespasses, as we forgive those who trespass against us.

Forgiveness, forgiveness. It is so difficult to forgive.

Pope Francis

19

AS WE FORGIVE

Every petition of the Lord's Prayer brings its challenges, but it is the forgiveness petition that presents the starkest, most obvious and, to many people, the most worrying challenge. 'Forgive us our sins as we forgive those who sin against us' is the way it is presented in modern language liturgies. And so it seems that just as the petition for daily bread was the only one to include an adjective, so this is the only one to include a condition. The condition being that *unless* we forgive others their sins, God will not forgive us our sins.

But is it really as simple and as stark as that? Do we believe in a God who waits to see whether or not we forgive others before forgiving us? Is the forgiveness of God a reward for those who are able to forgive, and denied to those who for whatever reason are locked in anger or resentment about what has happened to them – or indeed to someone else?

The short answer is, 'not at all'. The long answer is – well, read on …

Forgiveness is a deep and strange business and not easily captured by slogans and sound-bites; in fact, it's not often very adequately captured by sermons or chapters or even whole books – even big edited books with chapters written by a variety of different experts. The subject of forgiveness touches on realities that it is really difficult to be clear and articulate about. First, because hurt and harm, injury and violation, have complex causes and multiple consequences. And second, because forgiveness involves complex and subtle psychological and ethical processes. In particular, overcoming uncomfortable though legitimate feelings or reconciling contrary perspectives – most obviously the demands of justice on the one hand and the demands of mercy or love on the other. Forgiveness is a big, deep and challenging subject. It is not, however, one that can be avoided by those who pray the Lord's Prayer.

One Sunday morning when I was preaching at a church I had not visited before I spoke about forgiveness in a way that was intended to be sympathetic to those who have found it hard to forgive. As I stood by the church door afterwards, a member of the congregation approached me with the demeanour of someone about to issue a challenge. 'That's all very well,' she said, 'but every day we say in the Lord's Prayer "forgive us our trespasses [pause for emphasis] *as we forgive those who trespass against us*"!'

She was of course quite right. Those *are* the words. She could have added to her argument by mentioning that in Matthew's Gospel the following words also appear immediately after the prayer: 'For if you forgive others their trespasses, your heavenly Father will also forgive you; but if you do not forgive others, neither will your Father forgive your trespasses' (Matthew 6.14-15). And later, in Matthew 18, after Peter has asked how often he should forgive and offered the suggestion that seven times would be generous, Jesus ups the stakes and says, 'Not seven times, but, I tell you, seventy-seven times' (Matthew 18.21-22). Then comes the cautionary tale of the so-called 'unforgiving servant', who, having been forgiven a huge debt himself, is merciless in extracting the small debt that he is owed by an underling. When the forgiving master hears of this, he is most indignant and rescinds his forgiveness.

"'You wicked slave! I forgave you all that debt because you pleaded with me. Should you not have had mercy on your fellow-slave, as I had mercy on you?" And in anger his lord handed him over to be tortured until he should pay his entire debt. So my heavenly Father will also do to every one of you, if you do not forgive your brother or sister from your heart.' (Matthew 18.32-35)

There are people who take the plain sense of this to mean that you must always forgive those who harm you without question and as soon as practically possible. I recently came across an example when reviewing a book for *The Church Times*: 'The point is a simple one – the one who does not forgive others has no right to expect forgiveness himself or herself.'

'Whoa!' I thought. 'Can I stop you there for a moment?' But it was too late: the book was already in print and I was reviewing, not editing it.

My beef with that statement is not that it fails to have some truth in it, but that it picks up on the hyperbolic nature of Jesus' teaching and, quite unintentionally, creates not only a painful but a cruelly unfair impression in the minds of those people for whom the question of forgiveness is deeply difficult. That is, those people who have suffered severely at the hands of another person and are torn between the desire to be true to the reality that they can't forgive – not just because it is difficult to do so but because they feel deep down that it would be wrong to do so – and the equally strong desire to pray the Lord's Prayer with integrity. And it is such people who are always on my mind when I reflect on the forgiveness clause in the Lord's Prayer. For that reason, much of what follows seeks to address this muddle. I offer no apology. It urgently needs to be sorted out.

Before turning to the question of what forgiveness means to those who have suffered significant harm, however, it is right to say something about what the petition means in less extreme situations. My suggestion is that in such cases the message is reasonably clear and straightforward.

Plenty of people have said that Christianity is a religion of forgiveness, and there are many layers of meaning in that, one of which is that Christianity is not a religion that encourages you to 'sweat the small stuff' of morality or scrupulosity. Nor is it a religion that encourages us to keep records of wrongs or to hold grudges when we are slighted or overlooked.

When Jesus said that we must forgive seventy-seven or seventy times seven times, the meaning was that we should be relentlessly forgiving in our attitude towards others. The basis for this attitude is that we are living in a community that is ordered by the principles of love and where trust is expected and honoured. It is within such an environment that it is wrong to keep a record of wrongs, or to nurse a grudge, or to retaliate when we experience a minor injury, offence or insult. Such matters are largely irrelevant where there is love and trust and where everyone is committed to justice, kindness and mutual care. In such a community, where the default is that people are well intended towards each other and acting with sensitivity towards each other's needs, we should be readily forgiving.

It's vital to note that the harsh words in Matthew's Gospel about what will befall those who fail to forgive are not directed at those who have suffered a terrible harm at the hands of others but at those who are unappreciative of the generosity of others. The criticism is of those who are needlessly and ridiculously mean-spirited.

Forgiveness is relatively easy when we are harmed in a context where others are kind and good towards us, supporting us and forgiving us as necessary. If we fail to forgive under these circumstances, then unless there is especial malice or exploitation in what happened there, it must be because we are cutting ourselves off from this love and positivity. And it is this cutting off, or shutting down, that leads not to God casting us out – that's just a figure of speech – but to us alienating ourselves from God's forgiving grace by placing ourselves in the outer darkness of our own petty rage.

It is a different story, however, when trust and power are exploited, and where the vulnerable are left with the physical and psychological wounds of abuse. Here the anger is not petty rage but a heartfelt cry for acknowledgement and justice, and forgiveness is a very different prospect.

2 0

WEIRD CHRISTIAN THINKING

The phrase 'weird Christian thinking' is not mine. I have taken it from a book about forgiveness after traumatic events written by Sue Atkinson, in which she writes passionately about both her own personal experiences and those of others. The personal story that she relates in the book is that while still in shock after having been attacked, while 'still trembling and having nightmares', she was advised by a clergyman that if she did not forgive the person who had attacked her she would 'go to hell'.

Sadly, Atkinson's experience is not an eccentric one-off. Indeed, she offers several similar stories. The story of Richard, for instance, who was subject to sexual abuse from both parents, as well as violence, incarceration and neglect. When Richard joined a church, he was offered some counselling, as a result of which he went home and tried to discuss his abuse with his parents. They were unsympathetic and insisted that they had done nothing wrong. This made matters worse for him.

At this point, his 'counselling' suddenly takes another turn.

Max, the counsellor, insists that the only way ahead is for Richard to forgive his parents. Richard says that this is what he was trying to do. Max says he must try harder, because, 'Jesus won't forgive you unless you forgive your parents.' Richard replies that it might help if they said sorry. Max doesn't accept the point at all and responds: 'Well, they didn't say sorry, and if you don't want to go to hell, you must forgive them.'

Atkinson reports that Richard went back to his room, cried for days and decided to abandon Christianity. It's hard to disagree with her conclusion that people subject to pastoral care or counselling based on this 'weird thinking' are 'abused all over again'.

While I think that Atkinson is right to call this 'weird', it is not especially unusual, and it is often found in those branches of the Church where there is a desire for a distinctive, clear and radical understanding of the gospel message. These can be admirable ambitions. But it doesn't always work out well.

The novel *Women Talking*, by Canadian author Miriam Toews, is an account of an imagined conversation that takes place among eight women of the Mennonite community in Molotschna, Bolivia. The context for that conversation is a set of true events that took place between 2005 and 2009. Most of the men of the community had conspired to drug the women and girls, all of whom were illiterate because of the educational policy of the community, with animal anaesthetics. They then raped them. The men told the women that their assailants were ghosts and demons, but in the end one of the women found a way to outwit them and discover and expose the truth. The men were arrested, tried, found guilty and imprisoned.

The conversation that the novel records is set in a hayloft where women from three different generations gather two days before the men are due to be released from prison. As they talk it all through, they identify three options for themselves: 'do nothing', 'stay and fight' or 'leave'. 'Forgive' isn't listed as an option, but is contained under the heading 'do nothing'. As the narrator puts it: 'And when the perpetrators return, the women of Molotschna will be given the opportunity to forgive these men, thus guaranteeing everyone's place in heaven. If the women don't forgive the men ... the women will have to leave the colony for the outside world, of which they know nothing.'

Clearly, the understanding is that there is an obligation to forgive and that it is the equivalent of doing nothing – the default option.

A very different story, though one that hinges on the same understanding of an overriding imperative to forgive, concerns the Amish people of the Nickel Mines community in Pennsylvania. On 2 October 2006, a gunman ran into the local school and captured the children. He later shot 10 of them before killing himself. Five of the girls died, the others were seriously injured. Almost immediately afterwards, members of the Amish community went out of their way to comfort and support not only those who survived the shooting and the bereaved, but also, and particularly, the close family of the gunman – who, while not a member of their community, had lived nearby and was well known.

The atrocity attracted media attention, but so did the forgiving response of the Amish people. A book called *Amish Grace* was written about the event and what followed, and a movie was also produced. In several interviews, people from the community explained their actions in terms of the passages from Matthew's Gospel that I have already mentioned. 'We have to forgive him in order for God to forgive us.'

It is clear from this brief exposition of weird Christian thinking that it can lead to various different consequences. In the case of the 'pastoral' counselling of those who have been abused or traumatized, the consequence is re-traumatizing threats. In the case of the Mennonite community, it led to a demand for acceptance and passivity from the women. In the case of the Amish of Nickel Mines, on the other hand, it led to positive, pro-social and healing engagement.

This mixture of outcomes can, however, be explained, because although the actions of the Amish towards the family of the gunman are acts of exemplary kindness and must have involved a profound mixture of generosity and courage, they are not, actually or really, acts of forgiveness. The family members of the gunman had not rounded up, terrorized or killed those children. They were, as close associates of those who perpetrate horrendous atrocities often are, themselves hurt and damaged by it. As for the perpetrator himself: he was dead and, in human terms, forgiving the dead, while it cannot be taken for granted, is not at all the same as forgiving those who are alive and who have not yet shown any sign of repenting of what they have done to you – like Richard's parents – and who also remain a threat to you – as the men do to the women in the Mennonite community of Molotschna.

But if the Lord's Prayer's petition concerning forgiveness doesn't mean, 'you must forgive instantly, thoroughly and irrevocably, irrespective of what you have suffered', then what does it mean? Inevitably, to answer this will involve considering some words in more depth.

2 1

WHAT EXACTLY NEEDS
TO BE FORGIVEN?

Most English-speaking people who say the Lord's Prayer in its traditional form will be familiar with the phrase 'forgive us our trespasses as we forgive those who trespass against us'. Those who are more acquainted with a contemporary form will pray, 'forgive us our sins as we forgive those who sin against us'. However, if we turn to Matthew's version, we will read, 'And forgive us our debts, as we also have forgiven our debtors' (Matthew 6.12). In Luke we read a slightly different version again: 'And forgive us our sins, as we ourselves forgive everyone indebted to us' (Luke 11.4).

Many English-speaking people are surprised or even troubled to learn that the actual biblical words of the Lord's Prayer refer to 'debts' and not 'trespasses' or 'sins'. But, as English-speakers in Scotland, whose prayer is formed by the Book of Common Order of

John Knox fully appreciate, 'debts' really is the key word here; Matthew has it twice and Luke only once. We will address the question of 'sins' later, noting for now that in New Testament Greek the word and concept of 'debt' and 'sin' are quite distinct. At this point, our question is: where did trespasses come from?

It's an intriguing story ...

We pick it up by taking a quick look at the Latin Vulgate Bible and noting that it is faithful to the Greek, using the phrase, *debita nostra*, 'our debts', which was balanced by *debitoribus nostris* – 'the debts owed to us'. In Anglo-Saxon versions of the prayer the phrase *forgef us scylda* is found. *Scylda* is a translation of the Latin *debita* but carries the meaning of guilt, offence or sin, representing, perhaps, an important first step away from the concept of 'debt'.

In the twelfth century, a version dropped talk of debt altogether and became more concrete, using the word 'misdedis' or 'misdeeds': 'And ure misdedis thu forgyve hus / Als we forgyve tham that misdon hus.'

Moving on to the later fourteenth century, however, we observe that John Wycliffe, who was translating from the Latin of the Vulgate, reverted to the language of debt rather than that of deeds, using the words *dettis* and *dettouris*. Wycliffe also introduced the word 'trespass', but, importantly, he did not use this word in the Lord's Prayer itself but in the verse that follows: 'For if you forgive others their trespasses, your heavenly Father will also forgive you; but if you do not forgive others, neither will your Father forgive your trespasses' (Matthew 6.14-15). It's interesting to note that the Greek word translated 'trespasses' here is not the same as the word that appears in the Lord's Prayer and is properly translated 'debts'. The Greek word in question is quite reasonably translated 'false steps', and so 'trespass' is entirely acceptable in this particular case, though it is problematic in the prayer itself.

It was William Tyndale, however, writing in the early sixteenth century, who introduced the word 'trespasses' into the Lord's Prayer itself. In his original spelling it is: 'And forgeve vs oure treaspases, even as we forgeve them which treaspas vs.' Tyndale's choice of words has shaped the way in which English-speaking people have heard and used the prayer these last five hundred years! We might well wonder how his act of translation could have been so powerful.

It was not because his version was adopted in the King James or Authorized Version of the Bible of

1611. The word used there is 'debts', as it is in most Bibles, as we have noted. However, Tyndale's word *was* adopted in Cranmer's Great Bible of 1539 and also in the First Prayer Book of Edward VI in 1549. And there it has remained, 'forgive us our trespasses as we forgive those who trespass against us' being the words used in the *Book of Common Prayer* of 1662; a document that has had untold cultural impact and that remains the normative prayer book of the Church of England.

And *that* is why Tyndale's choice of 'trespasses' has been so influential. Not because it is an accurate translation, but because it is the version used in the Prayer Book. Day after day, week after week, for five hundred years English-speaking people have read, recited or repeated the words of the Lord's Prayer in this version: 'forgive us our trespasses, as we forgive those who trespass against us'. If ever an example were needed of the formational power of the words of Common Prayer, then this is it.

Whether or not 'trespasses' is an acceptable translation of a word that really means 'debt' depends on what you mean by 'trespasses'. If the thought is, to enter onto land or into property without the permission of the owner, as in 'trespassers will be prosecuted', then the meaning is not particularly close. However, the older meaning of 'trespasses', which according to the *Oxford English Dictionary* goes back to the late thirteenth century, is 'transgression', which might mean 'a breach of law or duty; an offence, sin, wrong; a fault'. This brings us to the question of sin; a word that has its own problems.

2 2

THE TROUBLE WITH SIN

Modern liturgical versions of the Lord's Prayer almost always use the word 'sin' or 'sins', although all those responsible for the publication of such prayers know that in Matthew's version of the prayer the Greek means 'debts'. As we have already noted, Luke does use the word 'sins', but only in the first part of the clause. If we want to follow Luke rather than Matthew, we should look to God for the forgiveness of our sins while forgiving others anything they *owe* us – any interpersonal indebtedness. I will argue that this is, in fact, a very helpful direction in which to go, but first we should consider the impact of what we have in contemporary versions of the prayer, where we refer to both our own sins against God and the sins of others towards us.

Sin is a high-octane religious word, but one not commonly understood or even accepted as a clear or helpful part of our vocabulary today. I once wrote a book about sin, and when interviewed about it on BBC Radio 4 was immediately asked why I had written about a word that most people considered to be either obsolete or harmful. 'To try to show that it isn't,' I replied, though I don't think the interviewer was convinced.

The reality is that 'sin' *is* a profoundly problematic word today. It is a very serious word in the Bible and in Christian liturgy, but outside that context it is often considered a kind of joke term, used to exacerbate the excitement of guilty pleasures in advertising, or trivial transgressions in comedy. My argument here, however, is the perhaps paradoxical one that life would not be quite so difficult if the word 'sin' had been altogether trivialized.

For most of Christian and Jewish history, serious matters have been discussed in the language of sin, and this still has a strong cultural echo. So although today sin mostly means 'trivial', 'naughty', 'perhaps worth a blush', but nothing more than that, it can still carry a sense of deep seriousness. For if something is really, badly, straight-up, no-giggling sinful, it is very bad indeed, close to evil in fact. And it is *this* sense of sin, not the 'naughty but nice' sense, that gets caught up with this petition of the Lord's Prayer.

Part of the problem is that the word 'sin' is repeated – we sin against God and others sin against us. We are accustomed to the repetition of 'trespass'; but that doesn't, in my view, cause the same sort of problem or inflict the same sort of spiritual damage, because trespass isn't a word associated with the more egregious or harmful things that people do. With 'trespasses' it's all about stepping a bit over the mark or getting a little out of line. Trespass isn't the sort of word that we reach for to describe the fault and its impact when someone has abused trust, inflicted serious harm or betrayed someone.

We see a sign that says trespassers will be prosecuted – but we cross the field anyway, hoping not to be noticed, and when we get to the other side we don't give the matter a second thought. Trespass is a good word for the everyday and significant but not deeply harmful moral transgressions that, as I argued in Chapter 19, we really should be quick to forgive if we are living in a benevolent and just society. Certainly we crossed the field, but we took care not to damage crops or disturb cattle, open gates or drop any litter. No harm was done, no one is any the wiser. Can such trespasses be easily forgiven? Well yes, of course, and whether or not someone confesses and repents is beside the point – though if we did run into the owner, we might admit what we had done; perhaps to clarify whether or not we might have permission to cross the field on a subsequent occasion. Some may argue that this is not true forgiveness, but that really is to quibble. The point is that no one holds on to the offence. We just let it go. And letting it all go is close to the root meaning of the Greek word translated 'forgive' here.

But the word 'sins' doesn't work in the same way as the word 'trespasses'. Sin is a polarized concept that invites people to think in extreme, limited and unhealthily binary terms. It's trivial – or it's an atrocity. So, if we could tune into the consciousness of someone praying this clause when the operative word is sins, we might hear something like this: 'Forgive me my trivial misdemeanours and my general inability to get anything quite right – fallen human being that I am – in the same way as I forgive … well … the person who abused me as a child and who still scares me to death; or the drunk driver who ploughed into me when I was cycling, causing an accident in which I was so maimed that I am no longer able to walk.' Or, 'Forgive me my failure to be regular in my prayer and not be as kind as I should be to my annoying mother, just as I have completely forgiven the man who raped me or the boss who bullies me or the ruling political party that systematically oppresses my people.'

Suddenly the weird thinking that Sue Atkinson has so clearly and bravely called out is presented in all its shame. The weirdness here is the notion that God would require those who have suffered extreme oppression or cruelty to forgive those who have hurt them as a precondition of any divine forgiveness at all. What sort of 'God' is that? A very different one to the father of the Prodigal Son and to the 'motherly Father' to whom this whole prayer is addressed. It would be hard to believe in the integrity and goodness of a parent, teacher or magistrate who, in order to encourage forgiveness, is prepared to punish those who have suffered harm so severe that they cannot, in their continued suffering, even imagine forgiving. Surely the first to be forgiven by any deity of love and kindness would be those who have been damaged by the hurt and harm inflicted by others, and who are struggling with the material, bodily, emotional and spiritual consequences of what they have experienced, together with a perhaps quite realistic fear that, given a second chance, the one who hurt them will do it all again.

The trouble with 'sin', then, is not so much that the word fails to connect with seriousness, but that it sometimes connects with the most horrendous things that we have experienced. We might think of our own sins as being our excesses of frivolity, but the sins of others are those aspects of what they have done that have hurt us the most. And to forgive these is a very different matter than the decision not to react excessively to the minor injuries and offences of everyday life – the 'trespasses', one might say, of others.

23

DIVINE PARDON AND HUMAN FORGIVENESS

In ordinary everyday language the word forgiveness is used quite broadly. For instance, it might refer to the giving up of anger and resentment towards a friend who harmed you for no good reason, or, perhaps, to the dropping of hatred towards a person whom you feel has caused a lot of damage and destruction through their arrogant and careless egocentrism. On the other hand, it might also be used in a situation where a person has transgressed the rules of an institution, been brought to account and found guilty, but then, instead of being given a serious fine or expelled, been offered a second chance. Philosophers have found it helpful to distinguish between these two cases, reserving the word 'forgiveness' for the first two examples – giving up resentment and anger and dropping hatred, and using 'pardon' for the second – where a guilty person is not punished. The decision in the latter is a legal one on the part of the state or other authority, not an emotional one on the part of the victim.

The distinction, then, is between forgiveness as the inner emotional development of a person who has been harmed, in which they 'let go' of retributive emotions, and 'pardon', which is the decision by an authority figure not to punish someone who is guilty. This distinction maps, I would suggest, reasonably closely onto the two parts of the forgiveness clause of the Lord's Prayer.

When we go to God for forgiveness, we are looking to God not to overcome bad feelings towards us, but to free us from the consequences of our offences against God – 'the guilt of our sins' as it is sometimes expressed. When, on the other hand, we think about forgiving other people, our thoughts are focused on how we might let go of our retributive emotions – resentment, indignation, anger – before they settle down as a grudge, bitterness or hatred. In other words, there is a real difference between 'divine pardon' and 'human forgiveness'.

Sadly – no, tragically – this difference is almost completely hidden in the Lord's Prayer as we know it. And this is a significant problem, as it suggests that either God forgives as we do or that we have the ability to pardon others as God does.

It would be wrong to say that this distinction was clearly articulated in biblical times, but there are hints in the Bible of more nuanced thinking about forgiveness. We find this not in Matthew's Gospel but in Luke's. To recap: Matthew's version, in its rawest translation, reads, 'And forgive us the debts of us, / as also we have forgiven the debtors of us.' Luke's, on the other hand, reads, 'And forgive us the sins of us, / for indeed [we] ourselves are forgiving everyone being indebted to us.' It is those who are indebted to us towards whom we hold negative and hostile feelings.

As we have already noted, whereas Matthew uses the word 'debt' twice, Luke uses 'sins' when it comes to what we ask God to forgive us and then refers not to those who have sinned or trespassed against us but to those who are 'indebted to us'. This is very much in line with the distinction between divine pardon and human forgiveness that we have just established.

A second difference between Matthew and Luke, found not in the vocabulary but in the grammar, makes things even clearer. Luke's version of the second clause reads, 'we are forgiving', whereas in Matthew it reads, 'we have forgiven'. In Luke the idea is of an ongoing action; not something that is cut and dried, over and done with, finished. There is the sense of forgiveness being something that is not a one-off decision, or quickly completed. The meaning, rather, is that it might have to be returned to again and again, because it takes time. This makes very good sense if we are talking about the human process of ridding ourselves of resentment, indignation, anger or even hatred towards those who have harmed us. But it makes no sense if it is pardon that we are talking about. Pardon is a matter of executive decision and once the decision is made the guilty party is set free.

In short, the two parts of the forgiveness clause in the Lord's Prayer refer not only to two different *agents* of forgiveness but to two different *kinds* of forgiveness. Use of the same word obscures this difference. Calvin's comments on this in *The Institutes of Christian Religion* illustrate the difficulty of making and maintaining this distinction.

> Finally, we petition that forgiveness come to us, 'as we forgive our debtors': namely, as we spare and pardon all who have in any way injured us, either treating us unjustly in deed or insulting us in word. Not that it is ours to forgive the guilt of transgression or offense, for this belongs to God alone! This, rather, is our forgiveness: willingly to cast from the

mind wrath, hatred, desire for revenge, and willingly
to banish to oblivion the remembrance of injustice.

There are genuine and abiding insights here, but
Calvin is, if I might put it this way, only half right. He
is correct to point out the difference between human
forgiving and God's forgiveness, and right to invite us
to engage with the question of 'will' here. We cannot
forgive unless willingly and yet willpower isn't always
sufficient to achieve forgiveness – and there are times
when it shouldn't be; when conditions are not yet
right for forgiveness.

However, we might demur when we read that he
thinks that we should be able 'willingly to banish to
oblivion the remembrance of injustice'. If a hurt goes
deep, or is traumatic, as we would now say, then the
memory of it is simply not amenable to deliberate
forgetting. Sometimes they may lie dormant within us,
but the sleeping dogs of resentment and indignation and
anger will not always lie still. And there are many cases
where they are right not to do so; when those who have
suffered should not acquiesce in the silence of injustice.

Calvin is even more wrong, I believe, when he goes
on to make complete forgiveness of others a *condition*
for God's forgiveness. 'For this reason, we ought not to

seek forgiveness of sins from God unless we ourselves also forgive the offenses against us of all those who do or have done us ill.' It's that word 'unless' that is so problematic, pointing towards a conditionality that is not consistent with the loving-kindness of our motherly Father. But having tasted the powerful logic of conditionality, Calvin savours it just too much and so goes too far. 'If we retain feelings of hatred in our hearts, if we plot revenge and ponder any occasion to cause harm, and even if we do not try to get back into our enemies' good graces, by every sort of good office deserve well of them, and commend ourselves to them, by this prayer we entreat God not to forgive our sins.'

It's another 'whoa' moment.

I can line up with Calvin if he means that we should neither allow hatred into our hearts, nor seek revenge or plot to hurt those who have harmed us – though we might accept that even confronting them with the consequences of what they have done may be a painful experience. But, like many theologians, Calvin runs too many things together here and fails to make space for the reality that there are situations in which forgiveness is not the best next step and circumstances in which it might actually be the wrong next step.

24

GRACE IN FORGIVING

The forgiveness clause in the Lord's Prayer is powerful and good because it connects divine forgiveness with human forgiveness. God's forgiveness is needed by any person who has a sense of sin – often experienced indirectly as regret over words and actions through which we have hurt or harmed others, shame concerning the ways we have let ourselves down, or the more general gnawing feeling of moral anxiety – traditionally called a guilty conscience. This forgiveness, the divine pardon of our motherly Father, is never withheld from us. Karl Barth is very strong on this point: 'What God's forgiveness is must be clearly understood. Here it is not a question of an uncertain hope, of an ideal to be sought or imagined. It is a fact. Even before I ask it, God has already granted his pardon. He who does not know that prays in vain. Forgiveness is already given, and this is the reality by which we live.'

When God forgives, we are pardoned – the guilt of our sin is eliminated and we are set free. God is eternally poised to free us in this way. Our role in the process is summarized by the word 'repent', which we can think of as shorthand for abandoning the ways of sin and embracing the ways of God. Or, as it is put when an ash cross is drawn on people's foreheads on Ash Wednesday, of turning away from sin and being faithful to Christ. Such repentance involves making amends for the harm we have done, and trying to put things right for those whom we have hurt and harmed; all this is encompassed as we turn to God and follow God's way.

God's forgiveness is not intrinsically difficult to access; it simply involves turning to receive it. Yet there is a difficulty here: the difficulty of turning away from the pleasures and compulsions of sin. Although the love of God is ultimately and eternally attractive, we often prefer the short-term yet ultimately self-damaging attractions of sin and succumb to temptation.

And yet our need is not only to receive forgiveness but also to forgive others. We need to do this for our own good; it is not healthy to carry all that resentment and simmering anger around. Contemporary psychology has discovered this truth and invested huge resources in seeking to find ways to help people forgive others. The insight is not a new one, however. Commenting on the Lord's Prayer in the seventh century, Maximus the Confessor is concerned about the inner peace and calm of the one who prays, repeatedly emphasizing the importance of 'detachment from passion'. He connects this with forgiving when he writes that 'the one who remains in detachment in what befalls him forgives those who have offended him, without allowing the memory of whatever painful [event] that has happened to him to be imprinted in his mind'.

Maximus seems to be suggesting the rather stoical stance of not letting insults and offences get to us. There is a place for developing a degree of resilience if we are to survive in anything but the kindest of environments, but resilience to offence is not the same thing as forgiveness, and this is a useless bit of advice to those who find that they have not so much been offended against as violated, and are traumatized day and night by what they have gone through. For such people, Maximus's conclusion, 'a pure disposition in regard to those who have caused pain is necessary for the mutual advantage of both ...', probably sounds like nothing more than fine words.

And yet there is much to be said for engaging in an effort to forgive those who have harmed us – provided that we have a realistic understanding of forgiveness as involving the gradual overcoming of both the hostility and the pain that we experience when others have offended, hurt, demeaned, insulted or violated us. Such forgiving is a tentative and precarious venture, yet even if it never ends it may still be authentic, admirable and important. What we need to be absolutely clear about is that embracing the way of forgiveness does not involve pardoning those who have wilfully, negligently, directly, or complicitly inflicted dreadful damage on us.

As is now clear, the forgiveness clause of the Lord's Prayer deals with extremely sensitive material in just a few words. We often make the matter more difficult than it needs to be by failing to differentiate between divine pardon and the word used for human attempts to forgive, obscuring the truth that human beings cannot forgive as God does, and thereby adding spiritual torment to the plight of those already suffering the disorientation, shame and degradation that result from severe kinds of harm and various forms of abuse. The care of those who have been deeply damaged by others may sometimes involve suggesting something of a forgiveness journey, but the Lord's Prayer is itself abused if it is taken to mean that unless a person can declare they have forgiven their abuser, God will never forgive them.

Does this suggest that we are 'off the hook' of needing to forgive others? By no means. In Marilynne Robinson's novel, *Gilead*, the ageing Reverend John Ames finds the text of a sermon he once delivered on this clause of the Lord's Prayer, connecting it with debt relief according to the Law of Moses and the story of the Prodigal Son. Looking back at the sermon he finds 'not much in it to regret' and feels that it concludes 'quite effectively'.

It says Jesus puts His hearer in the role of the father, of the one who forgives. Because if we are, so to speak, the debtor (and of course we are that, too), that suggests no graciousness in us. And grace is the great gift. So to be forgiven is only half the gift. The other half is that *we* also can forgive, restore, and liberate, and therefore we can feel the will of God enacted through us, which is the great restoration of ourselves to ourselves.

There is grace in forgiving, and much to be said for behaving like the father in the story of the Prodigal

Son, but there is, sometimes, grace in not forgiving but in retaining a non-hateful, non-vengeful indignation, and acting on a righteous and responsible desire to name the wrong and to call to account those who have abused their power. This is the grace of honesty and patience. Sometimes the grace of forgiving will have to wait until truth and justice have had their day.

Many theologians have argued that this petition really needs to be read in reverse, so to speak. Karl Barth put it like this: 'we are not faced with an exhortation, "Go forgive," but we are confronted by a simple recognition of a fact: When the pardon of God is received, it enables us to forgive'.

Psychologists and others will say that we need more than God's forgiveness to enable us to forgive, but the message for the Christian teacher, preacher and pastor is that human forgiveness flows not from fear of divine rejection but from a fresh understanding of the empowering grace of divine acceptance and pardon.

PART FIVE

TEMPTATION

And lead us not into temptation; but deliver us from evil.

The prayer began with the word 'Father', it ends with the word 'evil'.

Simone Weil

25

AVOIDING TEMPTATION

We have already seen that Gregory of Nyssa was an early and influential commentator on the Lord's Prayer. He took a particularly clear view of this petition and drew from it a very practical lesson. The natural reading of the petition today is that it has two aspects based on the two verbs 'lead us not' and 'deliver us from', but Gregory saw unity here because he believed 'temptation' to be one of the names of the devil – the ultimate source of threat and danger for the Christian soul. He had scriptural warrant for doing so. In 1 Thessalonians 3.5, Paul writes that 'I was afraid that somehow the tempter had tempted you.' For Gregory, to pray this petition is to take on board the practical advice of steering clear of the tempter and avoiding all sources of potential spiritual harm and corruption. He writes that 'we should be separated from the things that belong to this world'.

Having experienced a pandemic, people today are more than ever aware of the strategy of keeping a safe distance from possible sources of danger. The 'social distancing' and the personal protective equipment, the self-isolation, the shielding and the weeks of lockdown, were all designed to keep human beings apart and therefore away from possible sources of infection by Covid-19. The logic is simple and effective. If you don't get close to the virus, it can't infect you. Just stay at home; and at all costs avoid other people.

Some saw all this as 'the great pause' and found in it the re-emergence of some important values, such as kindness, a calmer sense of the passage of time, and a filtering out from our lives of the obsessions and false gods that, before most of us had heard of coronavirus, were undermining the good calm order of life and the ease of dignified contentment. Suddenly we were less worried about the fortunes of celebrities and were giving time to each other rather than to needless shopping trips. That was one side of it and for some people this would have been the main impact. For others the costs of the pause were considerable indeed, whether the loss of education for children, of healthcare for those suffering from any number of afflictions other than Covid-19, the impact on the family finances of not being able to run the business that puts bread on the table, or the effect on the national or global economy of not allowing many forms of production and trade to occur – not to mention those who became seriously ill or who lost a loved one to the virus.

Gregory's suggestion of avoiding temptation and evil by keeping a distance from 'the things of this world' leads naturally to a strategy of voluntary lockdown and withdrawal. There are many Christians who have taken this route, forming isolated communities, whether monastic or otherwise.

The strategy has its attractions for those who are anxious about temptation and evil, but has two fundamental flaws. First, that the dynamic of distancing is also one of disengagement. The members of the isolated community have a strong sense of fellowship – but it is limited to their own community. The many others of the human race may be respected, admired or even supported and helped (such self-isolating groups can have active welfare or charitable projects), but they are inevitably viewed with suspicion, for they have not chosen to isolate themselves from temptation.

The strategy has a second flaw too. The strategy of avoiding a threat can be a good one if the threat is clearly identifiable and its location has distinct boundaries. Gruinard Island in the west of Scotland is infected with anthrax. Other islands are not. The strategy of keeping safe from anthrax by not going to Gruinard is a sound one and not at all 'costly'. There are plenty of other islands off the north-west coast of Scotland to visit. When it comes to temptation and evil, however, it is far from clear that the analogy really works. Just because there are clear temptations in one context does not mean that there are no temptations in another. We might be able to identify temptation-rich zones, but we cannot expect to find any temptation-free zones. And we certainly cannot think of no-go areas for the devil.

There are some specific occasions when the strategy of avoidance is the right one to use against temptation. In particular, those who are afflicted with an addiction will know that it is best to keep their distance from alcohol or narcotics or opportunities to gamble. But this is a strategy based on knowledge of personal weakness and vulnerability – not on an analysis of where temptation or the devil might be lurking. In fact, no such analysis is possible. If it were, life would be very much simpler and less challenging than it is. We may seek to avoid the devil, but the devil won't be avoiding us.

The best response to temptation is not to attempt to avoid it altogether. That is an unliveable solution that ultimately turns us in on ourselves – itself a traditional description of what it is to be trapped in sin. Rather, we must learn how to live with it without being either frightened of it or overwhelmed by it. Avoidance has huge costs, and to put it bluntly, the kingdom isn't going to come (never mind the kin-dom) because people steer clear of temptations by avoiding 'this world'.

For most of us, most of the time, life is spiritually difficult in complex and subtle ways. Just as a burglar will not try to look like a burglar or carry a bag labelled 'swag', the tempter will not come to us dressed in a Satan outfit. The tempter works by stealth and the most difficult-to-resist temptations will be those that slip unnoticed into our minds and hearts using respectable channels, insinuating themselves into our most high-minded goals and aspirations.

This is the context for this clause of the Lord's Prayer. The previous one was realistically based on the appreciation that we would at the time of praying be in

God's debt because of our sin and failure. This petition involves turning our attention to the future and bringing before God our desire and intention not to run up such excessive debts in the future. It is focused on the dark and difficult side of the hours and days yet to come, and brings into focus the expectation that, as time goes by, we will get things wrong, embarrassing or shaming ourselves in the process and sometimes, alas, hurting, harming or betraying others. And we pray this petition not hoping that we will be able to avoid all temptation, but that we will sometimes, at least, not succumb to it.

26

LEAD US NOT

Astute users of the Lord's Prayer will have long since noted that this is the only instance of a negative in the prayer – the only time we ask God *not* to do something. And many – among whom, the current Pope, Francis, is the most celebrated recent example – have questioned whether this sort of negative prayer makes pastoral and theological sense. Surely, they protest, a good and loving God would never intentionally lead us into temptation. Why then should we spend time asking God not to?

However, the actual wording in the New Testament doesn't seem to support the Pope's view that we should avoid asking God not to do something that we don't believe God will actually do. The word translated 'lead' might mean 'to bear, carry, move, bring, lead or drag' – so there is some scope to re-translate it; but when we realize that it is the same word that is used to describe the actions of those who took a paralytic man to Jesus to be healed, we might think that 'do not lead us' is, if anything, too weak a phrase. 'Do not bodily drag us into these situations' might seem to be more like it.

Nonetheless, some Catholic European Churches have moved to a different form of words here. In Italian, the idea has been expressed that it means 'do not abandon us to temptation', and in French, 'do not let us fall into temptation'. Although it caused something of a stir in the media, the Pope's opinion is not a new one. In the early third century, Tertullian proposed the sort of wording that has been translated 'suffer us not to be led into temptation' and he was supported by his fellow north African, Cyprian of Carthage, a few decades later. But Augustine of Hippo, yet another north African bishop, and a man of extraordinary productivity and matchless influence, favoured the more succinct 'lead us not'.

Moving on a thousand years, we discover that no less controversial a figure than Henry VIII was an enthusiast for the approach that Pope Francis now advocates. The words 'suffer us not to be led into temptation' appear in a book issued in his name in 1543. Properly titled *A Necessary Doctrine and Erudition for any Christen Man*, it is more commonly known as *The King's Book*.

The king's view did not prevail in England, however, and the already traditional wording, 'lead us not', was used in the first and all subsequent versions of the *Book of Common Prayer*; which, as we have already seen, has proved to be the most influential document in shaping the way English-speaking people understand the prayer that Jesus taught his disciples.

It seems unlikely that this issue is going to be resolved in our lifetimes, but it might be worth clarifying the issues – as far as we can. The real problem here is that we have a negative petition in a prayer addressed to God. So we must ask whether it makes sense to ask a good God *not* to do something that we believe would have negative consequences.

One response to this is to point out that there are other biblical prayers that express things negatively. When we come across the words 'do not take your holy spirit from me' (Psalm 51.11), we do not imply that we believe that God has a plan to do any such thing. The point rather is to express our dread of the prospect. The meaning of the phrase is an expression of our own awareness of our reliance and dependency on the Holy Spirit. Positive and negative expressions are both part of the poetry of prayer. They may not represent beliefs or reflect convictions straightforwardly. Rather, they give voice to something deep within us, whether it's a delight or a dread.

The most helpful suggestion that I have found about this petition in terms of a direct meaning is found in John Nolland's commentary on the Gospel of Matthew. Nolland writes that it is a prayer 'to be spared times of great pressure, times that would prove very trying. The prayer reflects a sense of one's own frailty and limitation, one's vulnerability to situations in which one "is placed".' Nolland makes a connection here with Jesus' words to his closest friends in the Garden of Gethsemane, translating them as follows: 'Watch and pray, that you may not enter into [what will be] a trial [to you]' (Matthew 26.41). The passage goes on to refer to the willingness of the spirit but the weakness of the flesh. The prayer is an articulation of the fear that we may be overwhelmed or overcome by temptations or trials.

It is, in other words, not so much a prayer that God would desist from certain actions, or that God's will and purpose might be altered to accommodate our preference not to be challenged. Rather, it's a prayer of self-awareness from those who have come to appreciate that they may not be able to face or manage or cope with everything that the future brings. It's rhetoric and poetry, not theology, as is most prayer. It's a *cri de coeur* that comes when we see the future bounding towards us like a tsunami of chaotic complications, or a sandstorm of blinding and suffocating micro-particles, each one too small to notice but together more than enough to smother and swamp us.

'Lead us not' doesn't mean, 'don't take us there'. It's too late for that; the troubles and tribulations, tests and temptations, are already on their way. It means, 'don't just dump us there'; or, 'do not leave us to our own devices, for we fear that we will be overwhelmed and destroyed'.

2 7

TEMPTATION, TEST OR TRIAL?

What makes a temptation tempting?

A classic temptation might be defined as a predicament in which there are two possible outcomes: short-term satisfaction and long-term ruin or short-term frustration and long-term fulfilment. This is the sort of thing that Oscar Wilde had in mind when he quipped: 'I can resist anything, except temptation.'

However, the word translated 'temptation' in the Lord's Prayer doesn't necessarily mean temptation in this sense. It can equally mean 'trial' or 'test' and has this sense when found elsewhere in the New Testament. Such a test can be positive and productive, a useful challenge to have faced rather than a dangerous dilemma to have lived through. A 'test' in this sense is an experience that builds or establishes good character; it could be a hardship that has strengthened a person in some way but that might, if it had been addressed differently, have led to personal bitterness or to envy of those who were spared such deprivation.

So – does the prayer primarily concern temptations, or tests? There are problems with answering either way. If it is tests in the positive sense, then why should we pray to avoid them? They are designed to help us develop, prosper and flourish – what's not to like? But if they are temptations designed to catch us out by presenting short-term pleasure and hiding long-term negative consequences, why do we think they are of God? Surely even to whisper such a prayer is to suggest that God has the ethics of a drug-pusher.

This is obviously *not* what we believe. We may, however, think that there is a force, power or being out there somewhere who does behave like a drug-pusher – and that is the devil, or Satan, the biblical figure sometimes actually known as 'the tempter'. For most of Christian history people have had a robust and earthy sense of the devil as some kind of personality. It made sense as part of a worldview replete with angels and demons and spirits of all kinds. Many do not see things that way these days, believing that it is better to think in more reduced, scientific and psychological concepts.

Nonetheless, it is absurd to suggest that the devil is *not* a character in the New Testament. Moreover, the wording of the Lord's Prayer in Greek does not refer to evil in the abstract but in the concrete, possibly personalized form, 'the evil' or 'the evil one' being good translations of the two words that conclude the prayer in Matthew: *tou ponerou*. Luke is less clear about where trials or temptations come from, as he ends the prayer on the word 'temptation' and doesn't refer to evil at all.

John Calvin is among those who reflect on the question of temptation and testing, and he finds a solution in terms of the originator of our trial and challenges. 'But God tries in one way, Satan in another. Satan tempts that he may destroy, condemn, confound, cast down, but God, that by proving his own children he may make trial of their sincerity, and establish their strength by exercising it.'

There is a third possible way of reading this. This is the interpretation that thinks not of temptation and trials as life experiences that are always with us, but of a 'time of trial' that will be part of the great reckoning when all history comes to its conclusion – 'the final test'. This interpretation has perhaps become the predominant one influencing biblical translation and interpretation. The New Revised Standard Version, for instance, has the phrase 'do not bring us to the time of trial'. (The New International Version, by contrast, has the familiar 'lead us not into temptation' – though with a footnote explaining that 'the Greek for "temptation" can also mean "testing"'.)

This idea of the ultimate test or time of trial found its way into the texts of the Lord's Prayer to be used in church services prepared by the International Consultation on English Texts, an interdenominational forum charged with providing modern (you- rather than Thou-form) versions of the core texts of liturgies that could be used by all denominations. This line of the Lord's Prayer was the focus of a good deal of attention and variety, with the 1969 version reading, 'Save us from the time of trial', whereas in 1970/1 it became, 'Do not bring us to the test.'

Much could be written about the way in which different denominations and the wider public responded to these forms of words. In the Church of England it was the 1969 wording that became part of the experimental form of Holy Communion service known as *Series 3*, which was authorized from 1973 and used until 1980. It fitted in well with a growing scholarly appreciation of the apocalyptic emphases in the New Testament. Jesus and his followers did not expect life just to keep going for ever and ever, but fully anticipated that the end times would arrive before long. Elsewhere in the New Testament, especially in the writings of Paul, it is clear that the ethics and the spirituality he promotes are not intended for the long haul of generations, but for the near future, pending the end.

The experimental wording used in *Series 3* (might we dare to call it a 'test'?) did not prove to be successful, and when the Church of England issued its compendium of services known as *The Alternative Service Book* in 1980, the phrase 'do not lead us into temptation' was restored. And so it has remained in both traditional language and contemporary forms of the prayer in *Common Worship*, which replaced the *Alternative Service Book* in 2000.

The failure of the 'time of trial' experiment is an interesting one to analyse. Was it too alien an idea? Was it too much of a change in rhythm and feel? Or was it that there was a more deeply felt need for people to be able to pray for support in the face of those experiences that they think of as 'temptations' in this most regularly used prayer? The least likely argument is that the proposal was defeated on strictly theological grounds – or those of accuracy of translating; indeed, the scholars of the day were those who lined up to support the apocalyptic 'time of trial' version.

Nonetheless, there is a theological case to be made against the view that the petition refers to an ultimate 'time of trial'.

Although there is undoubtedly a strong apocalyptic strand in the New Testament, the Lord's Prayer itself is a prayer that is anchored in the here and now – 'give us *this* day …' It is a prayer to help us live in messy, ambiguous, ongoing time. Moreover, it is only if the prayer is about the actual testing and tempting that we experience in life that it can do any spiritual work for us. If it is a prayer that God will hold off the final trial until we feel we might be ready, it is, perhaps, only a slightly more meaningful act than crossing the fingers of our praying hands. And if God's plan is that there is to be a final time of trial, it would seem futile to put our spiritual efforts into adjusting its timing. If it is due next Tuesday lunchtime, then that is presumably when it will come, no matter how many people pray this prayer on Tuesday morning– or how earnestly. Better, therefore, that we pray we may not be overwhelmed by temptation before then.

28

THE EVIL ONE

Our reflections have so far circled around the idea that there is an 'evil one', a tempter who has the capacity to entice us to make bad decisions and to draw us away from God's will and way. It is time now to focus on this question: what are we to make of the idea that there is an 'evil one', which (or, should it be who?) is such a danger to us that we are invited to pray for deliverance from it (let's not get muddled up with gender here) as often as we are asked to pray for daily bread or the forgiveness of our sins?

Many modern people will feel some discomfort in thinking in terms of a personal devil. There are good reasons for this. First, there are those who might use the devil as the explanation of their actions and thereby seek to evade responsibility. Second, there is the sheer embarrassment experienced when others hear that we hold to such a childish or primitive view (especially if the devil is imagined with cloven hoofs and horns and carrying a pitchfork). Third, there is the more sophisticated concern of 'dualism'. Dualism is the belief that there is some kind of equivalence, or parity, between God and the devil; the one good and wise, the other malicious and cunning.

Let me address these three concerns. First, the problem of the devil as 'excuse'. While blaming others for our own failings is not good, it is often the case that the pathway that leads to an action is complicated and that many factors and forces are involved in leading us to a bad decision or action. We always therefore have the option of stepping back from our responsibility and finding something or someone other than ourselves to blame. However, the fact that we may over-blame one of a number of potential influencers on us does not mean that we need to deny their existence in order to ensure that we accept responsibility for our actions. It may be wrong to blame the devil for our faults, but our inclination to do so neither proves nor disproves the existence of the devil.

Second, the embarrassment issue. This can be quite acute for some people – and it is aggravated by the use of demonic imagery in the marketing of all sorts of products that might be regarded as 'sinful' – whether because they are self-indulgent or slightly risqué. Equally, the whole Halloween industry, designed to make fun out of a mixture of death and demons, only piles on the embarrassment for those who pray to be delivered from the evil one. But once again, the fact that something can be presented trivially does not mean that there is no underlying reality or anything serious there in the first place. The fact that people dress up as devils or describe trivial treats as demonic doesn't mean that there is, or is not, a real devil somewhere not very far away.

Finally, dualism – the notion that there are two more or less equal beings, one called 'God' who is responsible for all that is good and wonderful and true, and one called 'Satan' who is responsible for all that is evil. Dualism sees the universe as the battleground between the power of God and the power of the devil. It is interesting and important that the religion from which Augustine converted to Christianity, Manicheanism, was a dualistic religion. His rejection of that way of thinking has been hugely and rightly influential throughout Christian history, helping to inform rejection of this false philosophy by monotheists, who insist that God is one and that there is nothing comparable with God.

For a monotheist, this exceptional nature of God is intrinsic to God being God. Polytheists don't see things that way and are happy to identify any number of deities, some of whom may be a little shady, to say the least. The monotheist will always respond to this with a courteous dismissal of the possibility, believing that if God really is God, then God can neither be divided nor multiplied nor in any sense equalled. There is no anti-God called 'the Devil' or 'Satan' in Christian belief.

Nonetheless, a rejection of dualism is not sufficient reason to dismiss all talk of an 'evil one'. All that the rejection of dualism requires of us in this area is that we don't think that the devil is any way comparable with God. Opposed to God? Yes. Animated by different values? Yes. In some way on a par with God? Not at all.

29

FOCUSED NEGATIVITY

Believing in the reality of 'the evil one' is not a comfortable position today, even if it is not entirely discreditable. And yet it seems to make more sense of this clause of the Lord's Prayer if we swallow our scepticism and accept that we need to be protected from a source of negativity that would prevent us from responding positively to God's will.

The most helpful question to explore here is not whether or not an evil one 'exists', but what reality does 'the devil' represent in scripture and in Christian tradition, mythology and spirituality? And that reality is both more and less serious than we might think. It is far more serious than the campily costumed naughty devil of trivial temptations, but also far more credible than the devil as God's rival sibling who is hell-bent on malevolence, and the escalation of suffering, and the destruction of anything that approaches peace, truth and justice.

To talk of the evil one is to recognize that there is a threat, but that the threat is not to God but to us. The evil one is 'the devil' with a small 'd': not a rival to God, but a tormentor of our better natures; a denier of the self that we might become; the block to our full flourishing as a person of faith, hope and love. The devil is the personification not of abstract evil but of the temptations that beset us as individuals and communities. The devil is focused negativity that presents itself to our minds sometimes as dread, but mostly as temptation.

The devil is the voice that whispers to us the ambitions that will distort our priorities; the blind-spot on our moral compass; the tendency that we have to excuse our own egocentricity. The devil is our denial of those failings in virtue that are so obvious to those with whom we live or work.

Notice how negative this is. The devil is negative and deals in negativity and turns you away from God's love and God's purposes – and so it gets worse.

The devil is the voice that says, 'don't trust yourself'; that says, 'you are not good enough' or 'you can never be forgiven' and that urges you to hold on to those vague guilt-feelings and ensure that they will go with you to the grave. The devil is the bit of you that aggravates the spinning self-talk of anxiety and adds water to the smothering wet blanket of depression.

The devil isn't only busy ramping up our negative self-talk. There are good actions to stop, injustices to be perpetrated, sins to be encouraged. The devil is that grip on your wallet when someone needs your money; that clamp on your tongue when someone needs a word of encouragement; that dreadful aversion of the gaze when someone needs the eye-contact of kindness – just precisely now. The devil is that dullness of the mind that stops you reading the story of suffering in Yemen or Syria, the forgetfulness that wipes from your mind the plight of those who were in the news headlines just a few weeks ago, never mind last year. The devil is compassion-fatigue, moral cowardice in the face of the abuse of power and the weary conclusion that real responsibility lies anywhere other than with me. The devil is the prejudice that insinuates itself into our unconscious minds and the racism in our institutional structures. See how crafty it is, how difficult to notice.

These are just a few hints about the reality of the evil one. Of course we cannot adequately describe the devil or have any idea in what guise the evil one will next appear in our thoughts or dreams, aspirations or anxieties. But we can be sure of this. The devil opposes the grace and glory and goodness of God with the blunt instrument of negativity. The devil will never prevail, but the devil will be happy if the divine intentions for flourishing and fulfilment in the kin-dom of God are frustrated.

We rightly pray that God would deliver us from this evil one. And yet we also know that these thoughts and fears stem not from outside us but from within. That's what's so scary about it.

There is nowhere to hide from the tempter.

30

TEST BY VIRUS

Temptations are all those thoughts that would divert us from seeking God's kin-dom and trying to understand and be obedient to God's will. They are traditionally understood to originate in the evil one – in some malevolent intelligence that is not only close enough to our mind to influence and distort it but also distant enough to be not quite the person we identify with – the real or true me. However, while we can think of the evil one as external to our better selves, we need not follow the mythical so far as to suggest that there is an actually alien intelligence. The intelligence, the mental power and pure suggestiveness of the evil one, are all fuelled by our own thinking and feeling apparatus – our brains, our minds, our cognitive and emotional faculties.

Tests, on the other hand, are not so much thoughts as events or circumstances. These might impact on the whole of who we are but are largely external to us – objective realities that trouble and endanger ourselves and others.

The epistle of James begins with advice to early Christians, probably converted Jews, who were being tested not by negative thoughts or corrupted desires but by economic poverty. The advice they get from James is worth our attention too.

> My brothers and sisters, whenever you face trials of any kind, consider it nothing but joy, because you know that the testing of your faith produces endurance; and let endurance have its full effect, so that you may be mature and complete, lacking in nothing. (James 1.2-4)

This we immediately note is the absolute opposite of negative thinking. Life is difficult – well, that's fortunate because it will lead you to maturity and completeness. One word that catches my attention here is 'consider'. James is saying, 'when life is difficult, think of it in this way …' That is, he is encouraging his readers to appreciate that it's not what happens to us that is most important but how we think about it, understand it and thereafter respond to it. James thus creates the same space, the space for consideration leading to response, that those who offer counselling, psychotherapy or CBT seek to expand constructively. To summarize James here, you might say, 'when life gets difficult – don't react, try rather to consider the positives that might emerge'.

That is the way he suggests we respond to trials. Make the most of them. Have faith. Good can emerge!

He also has advice relevant to the experience of temptation.

> Blessed is anyone who endures temptation. Such a one has stood the test and will receive the crown of life that the Lord has promised to those who love him. No one, when tempted, should say, 'I am being tempted by God'; for God cannot be tempted by evil and he himself tempts no one. But one is tempted by one's own desire, being lured and enticed by it; then, when that desire has conceived, it gives birth to sin, and that sin, when it is fully grown, gives birth to death. Do not be deceived, my beloved. (James 1.12-16)

It is interesting to note James's emphasis on endurance both with regard to temptations and to trials. The importance of this is that temptations and trials all get their power from the tendency of the human spirit to be worn down over a period of time. We can cope with a great deal provided it doesn't last very long, or once we can see the light at the end of the tunnel. Trials and temptations tend to get the better of us when we cannot see to the far side of them, however. That's when we go under, or give up, or collapse or explode or flare up or burn out ... note the vivid and contradictory nature of the language we use in such situations.

When it comes to recent events, there can be no doubt that the greatest test humanity as a whole has experienced in recent decades is the Covid-19 pandemic. There is no deed to describe the extent or the detail of that modern plague here; we all know enough of the facts and have experienced at first-hand what it meant for us, our loved ones and our communities – and we will all, in different ways, live with economic, social and political consequences for many years to come. The question that is worth considering is the theology of the pandemic in general and in particular the question of how it relates to this clause of the Lord's Prayer.

The distinction between test and temptation that we have explored has proved to be a very helpful one. The pandemic and its consequences were and are a test, and have called from us the skills and attitudes needed to endure and survive. Whether or not we could ever consider it positively I find hard to imagine. Certainly I believe that each person's efforts to endure could have positive outcomes, but whether those positives sufficiently outweigh the suffering that was inflicted around the world is another matter.

The pandemic also had a huge impact on the opportunity afforded to the evil one – our own mind's negativity – to distract us from God's will and way, and to be the agents of our own harm and diminishment. Some will have been strong and steadfast in the face of these temptations; others will have capitulated to greater or lesser degrees. We all, with greater or lesser self-awareness, know our own stories.

Thinking about the pandemic and this clause of the Lord's Prayer in the same breath has brought home to me that it isn't helpful to think of such tests as coming directly from God. Rather, we should think of tests coming from reality. Reality is of course ultimately created by God in such a way as to provide both simple delights and formational tests and a range of experiences in between. However, that fundamental belief does not need to lead us to the conclusion that the Covid-19 pandemic was a divine device to teach humanity in general and individuals in particular a lesson.

We are tested by reality and tempted by the evil one – that evil one not being a peer of God but the negative and self-destructive aspects of our own thought processes that are triggered by our responses to reality. Some situations are more testing than others, and some are more laden than others with temptations – occasions on which we are enticed to make a decision or engage in an action that has significantly negative consequences for ourselves or others. There is no realistic way of avoiding reality(!) and that is why it makes good human spiritual sense to bring our fear that we might not be able to resist temptation or cope with excesses of potentially overwhelming trials in life into our prayer.

The traditional words of this clause are not perhaps the way in which we might today choose to express these matters, but the suggestion here is that when we say them we mean something like this: 'spare us any trials that would overwhelm us, and help us to resist the power of the tempter'.

PART SIX

GLORY

For thine is the kingdom, the power, and the glory, for ever and ever. Amen.

Glory is the final word of religion, as joy is its final state.

Evelyn Underhill

31

THE DOXOLOGY FROM
THE *DIDACHE*

I know that's a forbidding title, but all will be explained.

If you look up Matthew 6 in the Authorized Version of the Bible you will see that it includes a verse that reads: 'For thine is the kingdom, and the power and the glory for ever. Amen.' (v. 13). Familiar words, but look for that same passage in the New Revised Standard Version or the New International Version and you will notice its absence.

What's going on?

The facts are that this line does not belong in the Bible at all and was first added to the Lord's Prayer in a very early Christian document called the *Didache* or 'Teachings' that dates back to the first or second century. Scholars argue about precisely when the *Didache* was written and disseminated, but it was at some point in the first three centuries of Christianity.

The specific teaching about the Lord's Prayer in this text is that it is to be recited three times every day. Illustrations and images from the period indicate that Christians would pray with their hands apart and slightly outstretched, and with their eyes open and looking up. 'Hands together, eyes closed' is not the traditional posture of Christian prayer, although it can be a very convenient way of encouraging young children to stop wriggling and adopt an earnest kind of seriousness.

The Western and Eastern Churches see this addition, which has since the earliest days been called a 'doxology', quite differently. *Doxa* is a Greek word meaning 'glory', and is often used to describe the final verse of a hymn that ascribes glory to God, typically enumerating the three persons of the Holy Trinity. The final verse from the ancient Easter hymn 'Ye choirs of New Jerusalem' is a classic example:

All glory to the Father be,
All glory to the Son,
All glory Holy Ghost to thee
While endless ages run.
Alleluia. Amen.

Ascribing glory to God is a regular feature of Christian worship. When psalms or canticles are recited in the course of daily worship, they are usually followed by a short verse known as 'the Gloria'. 'Glory be to the Father and to the Son and to the Holy Ghost. As it was in the beginning, is now and ever shall be, world without end. Amen.' Or in more contemporary wording, 'Glory to the Father and to the Son and to the Holy Spirit. As it was in the beginning, is now and shall be for ever. Amen.' Another, far more extensive 'Gloria' is said or sung in services of Holy Communion; this is the '*Gloria in excelsis deo*' or, in English, 'Glory be to God on high' or 'Glory to God in the highest'. Although both are known in the West as 'Glorias', following the tradition of referring to Latin spiritual songs by their first word, they are also, stepping back to the Greek, doxologies.

In the Churches of the Orthodox East, the doxology of the Lord's Prayer is seen as integral to it and so is always included. This is partly because it appears in some early Greek versions of Matthew's Gospel, which are given higher status in the East than they are in the West, where the fact that most of the earliest manuscripts lack the phrase is given more weight.

The twentieth-century Estonian priest and theologian, Alexander Schmemann, calls this ending a 'solemn exclamation', enthusing that it is based on 'three key words and biblical meanings, three main symbols of the Christian faith'. And the French Orthodox writer, Olivier Clément, concludes his brief remarks on the prayer as a whole with this terse comment, '"For Thine is the Kingdom, and the Power, and the Glory," meaning the cross, the love and the life that is ultimately victorious.'

Attitudes in the West are less uniform and the doxology is sometimes in and sometimes out. It is not in the Latin Vulgate, although the word 'Amen' does appear, preceded by the grim word *malo* (evil). However, when Roman Catholics use the Lord's Prayer at Mass today it is often followed by another short prayer, intriguingly called an 'embolism' said by the priest alone, which, in turn, leads into a version of the doxology said by the congregation together.

As for the Protestant Churches, Martin Luther excluded it but John Calvin was a champion of the longer ending and included it. In terms of the Prayer Books of the Church of England, the doxology doesn't appear at all until 1662. But even in that book the matter is not quite settled and the longer ending is not always used. For instance, in the order for Morning and Evening Prayer we find the Lord's Prayer twice, the first with and the second without the doxological ending. In the order for Holy Communion, the Lord's Prayer also appears twice, the first time (when it is said by the priest alone) without the doxology and the second time (after all have received the sacrament and say the prayer together) it is with the doxology. That's Anglicanism for you!

Lancelot Andrewes, the Anglican bishop of Ely and then Winchester, who was involved in the translation of the King James or Authorized Version of the Bible, includes a sermon on this clause in a series on the Lord's Prayer without any pause for comment or explanation. He views them as the words of Christ and expounds them as scripture, noting in passing that Christ based the conclusion of his prayer on the words of David at the dedication of the Temple, 'Thine, O LORD, *is* the greatness, and the power, and the glory, and the victory ... thine *is* the kingdom' (1 Chronicles 29.11, Authorized Version).

Even more interesting is that Andrewes sees the Holy Trinity represented here. 'These words, Kingdom, Power, and Glory, being jointly considered, are a representation of the Trinity.' He goes on to write that: 'If we consider them severally, although they may all be ascribed to any Person of the Deity, yet "the Kingdom" is to be ascribed unto Christ, "Power" to the Holy Ghost, and "Glory" to the Father …' To Andrewes, this final phrase of the prayer is doxological in the most thoroughgoing sense of praising the Trinitarian God in its completeness.

Slight differences aside in the way in which it is used in the Roman Catholic liturgy of the mass, and excepting the fact that in the *Book of Common Prayer* services it is only included on one of two occasions that the prayer is said or sung in each service, the doxology has now been universally adopted and is used and experienced as an integral part of the prayer.

32

ULTIMATE FULFILMENT

Including the doxology gives the Lord's Prayer an ABA or 'envelope structure' so that the end is more like the beginning than it is the intervening material. This is not an uncommon shape in Christian prayers and poems, and is often found in the Psalms.

If we compare the opening and the closing words, however, we find that the opening has a more personal and intimate feel to it. 'Our Father ...' is a warm and affectionate phrase, whereas at the end the address is more abstract, whether it is the traditional, 'thine is', or the modern, 'are yours'. We might see this as an aspect of the spiritual journey on which the prayer guides us – from God as loving parent to God as completely transcendent being who is all power and glory. We might imagine it as a journey through a funnel in reverse, from the narrow tube at the bottom to the wide opening at the top. If that isn't a winning or poetic image for you, then picture it instead as the journey from the trickle of a pure and welcome spring high on a mountain to that point where a splendid estuary spills out into the endless enormity of a mighty ocean, the scale, depth and grandeur of which we can hardly imagine.

It was with such an image that the Victorian Anglican poet and priest John Keble concluded his hymn, 'Sun of my soul, Thou Saviour dear': 'Till in the ocean of thy love / we lose ourselves in Thee above.' These are Keble's original words, though in many hymn books the word 'heaven' replaces 'Thee'. It is the word 'heaven' that is perhaps closer to the sense of moving towards a limitless presence of God that we find in the doxology of the Lord's Prayer than the more focused sense of God that the word 'Thee' suggests, which fits better with the 'Our Father' of the beginning.

This oceanic imagery is a very long way from the sort of thoughts and feelings and pictures that immediately come to mind when we think of 'kingdom'. We explored that word in some detail when considering the second clause of the prayer, and found it to be too unhelpfully laden with a sense of hierarchical 'power over' to serve its intended spiritual purpose. We do not need to rehearse those arguments again here. However, while the neologism 'kin-dom' is a useful jolt to the imagination, it is not the only word that might speak for us today of the kingdom that Jesus announced. In particular, the word 'fulfilment' suggests itself as something that might indicate the sort of trajectory of life that is intended here.

As we ponder the final words of his prayer, and imagine where the whole thing is taking us, bearing in mind that the early church teaching manual, the *Didache*, instructed its readers to pray this prayer three times every day, might it not be reasonable to hope that it is taking us towards fulfilment. But not just any fulfilment; rather, God's fulfilment: 'for thine is the fulfilment ...'

What, then, might God's fulfilment of us be?

It is interesting indeed that the prayer that Jesus taught us offers little scope for us to offer to God our own plans and projects, our own sense of needs, wants and desires. The petitions in the prayer are for bread, forgiveness and that we won't be overwhelmed by tests or temptations. That's it. So it would seem that the sort of fulfilment that God has in mind is fairly simple. There is no space for anything fancy, exotic or fussy. Moreover, there will be nothing exceptional about it. There is no suggestion here of a differentiated heaven – or of various qualities, never mind quantities, of reward for those who have lived more or less well. The justice of eternity, Christianly understood, is profoundly egalitarian, being fuelled not by judgement, but by mercy.

The Christian task, the most important work of spirituality or discipleship, is not to try to achieve our own fulfilment, never mind to earn our place, but to get ourselves into a position, to adopt the disposition, of ever more open acceptance of what God is pleased to give. In parallel with this is the work of developing less and less interest in those things that do not come from God or that, if we engage with them inappropriately, draw us away from God. But alongside this comes the question of power. How does power relate to fulfilment?

33

POWER – BUT WHAT SORT?

The question of power is rather a large one to encounter at this stage in our journey through the Lord's Prayer. Not that we are unfamiliar with the idea of God being powerful – many of our prayers are to 'Almighty God'. And when in Chapter 5 we reflected on 'who art in heaven', it became clear that the phrase does not mean 'who is remote and irrelevant' but rather, 'who is present and powerful'.

What then can we say about the sort of power that is all God's and that informs the positivity that attends to this added end to the prayer that Jesus taught his disciples and that they, in turn, have bequeathed to us?

The answer to this has to be informed by the way in which we see power manifested in the life and ministry of Jesus Christ. The most obvious thing to say is that Jesus has personal power – he attracted a dedicated band of individual followers and significant crowds to hear his message. In the end they all deserted him, but even then they remained together after his death. Even in his absence they were loyal to bonds of commitment that had been built up under his leadership. He certainly had power of presence (think of him standing silently before the bumbling Pilate in John 19) and was capable of powerful utterance. His statements often provoked questions and sometimes his answers silenced the questioners; most categorically when the Pharisees set a trap for him.

> 'What do you think of the Messiah? Whose son is he?' They said to him, 'The son of David.' He said to them, 'How is it then that David by the Spirit calls him Lord, saying,
>
>> "The Lord said to my Lord,
>>
>> 'Sit at my right hand,
>>
>> until I put your enemies under your feet'"?
>
> If David thus calls him Lord, how can he be his son?' No one was able to give him an answer, nor from that day did anyone dare to ask him any more questions. (Matthew 22.42-46)

It is true that Jesus sometimes exercised power in a direct and rough way. He had a sharp tongue when it came to denouncing religious hypocrites and was trenchant in his criticism of those who prioritized obedience to the letter of the law over mercy and loving-kindness. But in these cases his protests were not delivered from on high but from below. The way in which he exercised power in this regard was so blunt as to antagonize people and to put himself in danger. He was a critic who, as he expressed his conscience and his passion, became ever more vulnerable himself.

It was when dealing with evil spirits, demons and the like that Jesus exercised power in a directly authoritarian way. Demons recognized him and begged him to let them be. In this area, the area where malevolence and negativity were doing their destructive work, he stepped in, stopped it and sent them away.

If these brief paragraphs give a sketch of the way Jesus exercised power, and if Jesus presents to us our best understanding of God, then we can say two things about the power to which we refer in the Lord's Prayer.

First, that the power of God is an absolute and unrivalled power when it comes to dealing with the forms of focused negativity that conspire to eliminate flourishing, joy and glory. God in Christ simply dealt with every such focused incident that crossed his path.

This is impressive power, but it is not the power to act so much as the power to prevent negative action on a small and localized scale. The double negative here isn't meaningless, because meaning, like fulfilment, requires the cancelling of negativity.

When it came to the aggregation of forces of negativity such as were found in the growing antagonism to Jesus and his cause among the religious authorities, and the weak leadership of the brutal Roman occupiers, Jesus was, however, powerless. Faced with the power of empire and religion gone wrong, there were no individual evil spirits to be rebuked, no subtle temptations to resist; the opposition was in deep-seated cultural and political realities whose power could not be constrained.

What are we to say then of the 'power' of God in Christ when he faced the powers that be in Jerusalem? It is here that we must either concede that Jesus represented a lesser power or find a perspective that reveals that Jesus was exercising and representing a *different kind of power*.

Faced with apparently insurmountable and antagonistic powers, Jesus did not resort to anything that looked remotely like a competition; he did not allow his response to be framed by what he was facing. His calm, dignified and contradictory silence before Pilate itself speaks volumes to any who find themselves facing the fearful guardians of aggregated powers.

We are in the realm here of the power of integrity and the power of deep, intuitive truth born of our experience and that comes from our life story. It is power that cannot be disconnected from vulnerability. This is the truth and integrity that makes 'power over' such an irrelevant matter when it comes to the deeper meaning and purposes of life. This is the sort of power that Michelle Obama is so skilled at helping black women to discover when she engages with them, saying, 'Your story is your power – own it and live it.' This message, given to those who have struggled with disadvantage, duties of care for family members, finding time for their own education and challenging inherited racism, is a vivid example of the empowering exercise of power. Gently offered, it encourages personal power that is peaceful, positive, good and is neither domineering nor controlling, but aligned to values of mutuality and service. It is rooted in honesty about both vulnerability and potential. It is unfeigned, genuine and self-aware. In a word, it is authentic.

The strange thing about this sort of power is not that it is so easily lost – but that it is so rarely found. Everyone has a story and many have stories of disadvantage, of being subjected to prejudice or oppression or exclusion. Such stories have two possible dynamics. First, there is the 'and so it continues' dynamic, in which the oppressed and rejected internalize that narrative and live it out. Second, there is the 'we shall overcome' dynamic. It is this second dynamic that can be liberated when those who have known and felt the story of rejection and exclusion can reach into the alienation and disempowerment of others and say, 'you matter'.

In her autobiography *Becoming*, Michelle Obama tells us that she took a group of 37 underachieving girls from Elizabeth Garrett Anderson School in London to Oxford University for a day, brought them to a gothic dining hall and, in the company of students and professors, said, 'All of us believe you belong here.' A study showed the power of her intervention. The students jumped from an average 'C' performance to 'A' after she started 'connecting with them', as she put it. Her message to the disempowered young is always the same: '*You belong. You matter. I think highly of you.*'

It is this sort of power, self-giving and other-affirming that should come to mind when we say the doxology of the Lord's Prayer. It's not the power of might or force or capacity to control, but the power that is good, generous and peaceful. The fact that the demons flee away when they encounter it is not because they are confronted, so much as because they are ignored, overlooked. 'When they go low, we go high' is a phrase the Obamas use to encourage each other not to be dragged down to the level of certain kinds of politicking. It represents the best way to respond to many of the demons that beset us, which depart because the space has been cleared of the material with which they work — negativity, despair, blame-seeking and the easy capitulation to the most self-defeating thought of them all: that the worst that has happened to me will inevitably shape my future.

This is the power of the motherly father whose very life is one of ever-extending, healing, forgiving and transformative love. This is the power that God not only owns but gives and in which we can share when we are prepared to allow the story of what has almost, but not quite, defeated us to become the energy whereby we reach out to others with the affirmation that, despite all that has happened, despite the way it seems, they too may come to ... Well, 'glory' might be the right word.

34

GLORY

Glory and power are not entirely separate categories in biblical thinking; they interconnect and overlap and are both related to sanctity and holiness. This is evident in the artistic and iconographic device of a halo – that sometimes all-too-deliberate attempt to signal a radiance that is more and better than merely human, and that shines forth from those on whom God's presence has settled.

Glory is intrinsic to God. We don't usually say this, preferring to think of love as the most enduring quality when it comes to the deity. But it can be helpful to speak of the glory of God as a constant because it reminds us that God's self-revelation is not something that happens from time to time, as if there is an on–off switch that can be applied to the divine nature. When we speak of God's glory we are referring to the unchanging, untiring, eternal extraversion of God; to God's relentless self-giving that, when we glimpse it, is the deepest and dearest beauty that is not only 'deep down things', as Gerard Manley Hopkins put it, but on the surface of things and shot through things. God's glory is extraversion that reflects the deepest integrity; it is not a show or a performance or even a self-presentation, but the outward flow of an inward truth.

In other words, God is the absolute opposite of a black hole.

Let me explain what I mean. We have grown accustomed to the summary of Darwinian evolution that is captured in the phrase 'the selfish gene'. Like all metaphors it can be both helpful and unhelpful in its application, but if you are convinced that a gene can be 'selfish' then you will be mightily impressed by the endless 'egocentricity' of a black hole, where infinite gravity pulls everything to its centre – from which nothing ever returns. A black hole cannot and will not ever *give* anything. It is the epitome of gracelessness. It has no glory at all. And as such it gives us a picture of the very opposite of God – who is all gift, all grace, all contribution, all love and all glory. Where a black hole sucks in, God breathes out; where a black hole destroys life, God gives life; where a black hole intensifies to the infinite, God extensifies to the infinite.

The glory of God is therefore nothing to do with the renown that is given to a human champion – whether it is prowess in athletics, business, art or academics that is being rewarded. Glory is not a prize. Glory is not gold or glamour or glitz. There is nothing of bling about true glory. Nothing of 'statement'; there is no 'signalling'. It is something that shines through. Glory is not self-conscious or presented. Indeed, self-presentation is something that all too often shades the little bit of genuine glory that a person might reflect. Which is why boasting can be so counterproductive, and why bragging has no place in discipleship or ministry. It may not kill glory, but it can put a significant shadow over it, maybe even eclipse it.

'Thine is the Glory, the self-revealed splendour of the Eternal Perfect filling and transcending creation; seen in its humblest beauties, yet never fully known.' These are the words of one of the most remarkable Anglican women of the twentieth century, Evelyn Underhill. She was talking about the doxology of the Lord's Prayer in the 1930s. Underhill was converted from youthful agnosticism to Anglicanism and became a hugely influential writer and speaker. Her focus was always on God.

'God is the interesting thing about religion, and people are hungry for God', she wrote in a sharply assertive letter to the Archbishop of Canterbury, bewailing the lack of spiritual depth in the clergy and calling for 'a greater interiority and cultivation of the personal life of prayer'.

Underhill encourages us to understand glory as the 'Beauty of God', not in a merely aesthetic way, as if God is extremely pleasing to behold, but rather as something that is revealed in the face of the crucified: 'Absolute Beauty is seen in the sacrifice of the Cross; the Perfect, the Strong, the Radiant, self-offered for the sinful, the murky, the weak, and achieving His victory through suffering, failure, death'. Clifton Black makes a similar point in his extended commentary on the prayer when he refers to the paradox that 'divine glory, visible to mortal eye, condescends to the deepest pit of human suffering and death, to the shaft of hell itself'. A place of suffering can certainly be a place of glory. Indeed, there are no situations from which the glory of God is banished. Occluded? Yes. Shaded? Yes. Eclipsed? Well, yes; but never finally eliminated, banished or destroyed. That is the meaning of the resurrection. The lights went out on Good Friday, but it wasn't long before the light of Christ was flickering again – no matter how improbably. Such resurrection is seen whenever the Spirit breathes new life into one who has succumbed to self-destroying temptation or been crushed by overwhelming negativity.

This is the same pattern that we saw when we considered 'power'. The power and the glory of God are awesome, but neither is a cause of anxiety because they are expressions of loving generosity and the sort of personal empowerment that facilitates the growth of a loving community. Such power and glory cannot be disconnected from joy. Evelyn Underhill understood this well and expressed it with apt economy and beauty.

Glory is the final word of religion, as joy is its final state. The sparks and trickles of the Supernatural which come to us, the hints received through beauty and through sacrifice, the mysterious visitations and pressures of grace reaching us through the conflicts, rebellions and torments of the natural world – all these are earnests of a Perfection, a Wholeness yet unseen: as the small range of sound and colour revealed by the senses witness to the unseen colour and unheard music of a Reality which lies beyond their narrow span.

Glory refers to what we see and what we do not see of God; our task is to so respond to it that not only do we learn how to see it more clearly, but we also find how to live in such a way as to obscure it less.

35

AMEN

The word 'Amen' exists in various forms in Semitic languages, and is always a form of assent or affirmation. It means 'yes' or 'I agree' or 'so be it'. Often in public prayer it is the only word said by the congregation, the others being read or extemporized by a minister. In the case of the Lord's Prayer, it is most unusual for the prayer not to be said by the congregation together, and when the gathering is multi-lingual, the prayer may well be said in several languages at the same time. The one word that all have in common on such occasions is the final one: 'Amen'.

Amen – the word betokens collective agreement as well as personal assent. It is certainly a 'we' word, at least as much as it is an 'I' word. It means not only 'I agree' but also 'and so say all of us'.

Having explored the prayer in such detail and at such depth, it seems only fair to offer some kind of summary.

Reader, I've rewritten it.

Motherly Father of us all,
    we honour and worship your being.
Your kin-dom come,
Your will be done
    at all times and in all places.
Give us each day the provisions we need.
Take away the guilt of our sin
    that we ourselves may be forgiving towards
    others.
Spare us any trials that would overwhelm us
    and help us resist the power of the tempter.
For in you is true fulfilment, authentic power and
absolute beauty.

It is not a translation, but an attempt to capture some of the truth of the prayer that is perhaps less obviously revealed in the familiar versions.

I wonder whether, having shared this journey of exploration of the prayer that Jesus taught us, you are able to add to it your own 'Amen'.

36

THY WILL BE DONE

Astute readers will have noticed that there was no exposition of this clause of the prayer in Part 2, 'Earth'. All the emphasis was on the kingdom – or rather, kin-dom – of God. Even more astute readers will have noticed that while my paraphrase of the Lord's Prayer in Chapter 35 changes almost everything, in this phrase the only change is the most minimal: from 'thy' to 'your'. And all but the most inattentive of readers will have noticed that these words are also the title of this book.

The reason for all this is that the conclusion I have come to is that it is in this petition that we find the essence of the Lord's Prayer – and indeed the essence of all prayer.

We may think that the point of praying is to inform God of the terrible circumstances in which people on our minds now find themselves, or to put God in the picture regarding our own deepest desires, or to update God on the extent to which we have succumbed to temptation and fallen into sin. We may think that if there is any persuading to do in prayer then it is us who will be twisting the divine arm and generally pointing God in the right direction. All this, however, is quite wrong.

In more positive moods we might think that if we praise God, extend ourselves in worship, go out of our way to write words and music of glorification, and offer them with all our heart and art, then we are in some way adding to the glory of God. This, however, is not right.

Yes, there are pious figures of speech that suggest this is the case, encouraging us to think that we might 'magnify' God's glory; but these are always and only figures of speech. J. S. Bach may have signed off all his compositions with the letters AMDG, to signify, *Ad Majorem Dei Gloriam,* meaning 'for the greater glory of God', but by the time the Mass in B Minor, for instance, had been composed and performed, the glory of God had neither increased nor decreased. The glory of God is just not that sort of reality. It is constantly and eternally, infinite glory. Does this mean that the B Minor Mass achieved nothing? Of course not. What it changed, or perhaps 'enhanced' is a better word, is the human awareness of that glory and the human capacity to respond to it and reflect it.

One of the themes of this book, not least the forgiveness section, is that human beings get things very wrong if they do not recognize that God is different to us in subtle and profound ways. This does not mean that we cannot use the language of human relationship and feelings when speaking of God, but we need to remember that when we do this we are trying to use words to do something that they are not quite able to do.

It's like trying to get our eyes to see the infrared and the ultra-violet at the upper and lower edges of a rainbow. We may try, but it isn't going to happen, however much we squint. They remain invisible and yet are definitely there – and so we use strange made-up words to 'describe' them, and think of them in terms of the colours that we can see; so the one is 'a bit redder than red', and the other 'a bit more violet than violet'. We might think of God as infra-loving or ultra-forgiving – but again, to do so would be to make a mistake. God is *completely* loving and forgiving; it is we who are inevitably deficient in these and any other qualities that find their perfection and completeness in God. There really are limits to what we can do. We are not God – an obvious point, but to remember it and understand it is to come both to a fuller understanding of God and to a form of humility that is realistic and ennobling; for it is in our actual, limited, humble humanity that we find both our need of God and our true dignity.

Prayer, ultimately, is the human attempt to embrace, and learn how to live with, the God-ness of God. This involves awareness of the extent to which God is like us, but also, and more importantly, the way in which God is unlike us. This embracing involves two aspects: the 'static' and the 'dynamic'.

On the 'static' side is our relationship to God's eternal nature as motherly father, God's 'heavenly' potency and presence, and God's glory. These all call for our affirmation and for responses as diverse as enthusiastic charismatic praise, perfectly ordered choral liturgy and the wordless silence of contemplation. In all these we may think we are making a personal contribution to the cause of divine splendour – but in reality we are not. At best we are just reflecting a little bit of what eternally is. We do not in fact glorify God; God glorifies us. If we ever shine, it is with borrowed or reflected light.

On the 'dynamic' side, we are relating to God's purposes and intentions – the ends that God has always had in mind for the creation that was brought into being by love and for love. This is the aspect of prayer that connects with the coming of God's kin-dom, the advance of justice, peace and truth, the provision of daily needs, the forgiveness of our own sins, our protection from harm, our resisting of temptation and our own reaching out in compassion, love and forgiveness towards neighbours and enemies alike.

'Thy will be done.' The phrase precisely summarizes this dynamic side of the prayer. When we say it we are praying that we might be enabled to go with the grain of God's intentions, in matters where we have the capacity to make a decision, or act, or hold an attitude. Another way of putting this is to say that we seek to fit in with God's law – always recognizing the way in which law is critiqued and developed in the New Testament and remembering that a word like 'way' is sometimes more helpful than 'law'.

'Thy will be done.' The point of the prayer is not to say a few words that mean that we vaguely acquiesce to the unfolding of some sort of divine plan over time, but that we give ourselves to understanding God, to affirming God, and to doing what we can to see if we can catch a few rays of glory and reflect them both back to God and towards our fellow creatures. In particular, it means that we do not remain neutral about God's will but make it our own.

'Thy will be done.' The word 'will' here does not refer to a particular line of thought or a decision to go along with a certain plan or project. The word is deeper, a matter less of 'head' than of heart and guts and motivation. 'Thy will be done' – may thy desires be fulfilled; for they are the most high-minded, most just, most inclusive and most dignifying of desires. When we pray that God's will be done, we pray that in our deepest depths we might be at one with the God who created us all, who loves us all, and who continues to inspire us all to a quality of fulfilment that we can as yet barely imagine.

'Thy will be done.' There may come a time when this is all we need to pray or all we can pray. There are times when it comes easily; when we can see the blessings that will flow from following in God's direction. And there are times when it will only come as the result of a tumultuous struggle with the captivating charms of our own self-will. As Simone Weil put it with typically devastating clarity and succinctness: 'We should ask nothing with regard to circumstances unless it be that they may conform to the will of God.' It's as simple and easy as that – in theory. The lived reality can be different, for all of us. For our tendency is always to be consumed by our own will, our own needs, our own desires. And yet ...

'Nevertheless not my will, but thine, be done' (Luke 22.42, Authorized Version). This was Jesus' most hard-won and decisive prayer, concluding his struggle with God in the Garden of Gethsemane. It was there too – in reverse – when he struggled with the devil in the wilderness: 'Not your will, Satan, but God's will is going to shape my life from here on in ...' We all want comfort, power, preservation and personal importance – but God's will is something of a different order. It is the divine desire for all that is best; for everything that will fulfil not just me, but all of us.

Our best prayer is that we might ultimately come to will what God wills. When we pray the Lord's Prayer, we believe that we are praying as God wills us to pray. And that is both a good start and a perfect end.

NOTES

Quotations from the Bible are from the New Revised Standard Version (NRSV) or Authorized Version (AV). Where no other version is mentioned they are from the NRSV.

INTRODUCTION

'richly ambiguous' ... Kenneth Stevenson, *The Lord's Prayer: A Text in Tradition* (London: SCM Press, 2004), p. 3. See also his *Abba Father: Understanding and Using the Lord's Prayer* (Norwich: Canterbury Press, 2000).

PART I

If we call our Father ... Gregory of Nyssa, *The Lord's Prayer, The Beatitudes*, translation by Hilda Graef (New York: Paulist Press, 1954), p. 40.

CHAPTER I

Father of us in the heavens ... In order to give as raw a rendering of the Greek as possible I have used the direct translation found in *The New Greek-English Interlinear New Testament*, translated by Robert K. Brown and Philip W. Comfort (Carol Stream, IL: Tyndale House Publishers, 1990), p. 19.

CHAPTER 2

motherly father ... See Gerald O'Collins, *The Lord's Prayer* (London: Darton, Longman and Todd Ltd, 2006), pp. 29–33.

the word 'Father' ... Joachim Jeremias, *The Prayers of Jesus*, quoted by C. Clifton Black in *The Lord's Prayer* (Louisville, KY: Westminster John Knox Press, 2018), p. 72.

gave the image a very homely twist ... O'Collins, *The Lord's Prayer*, p. 29.

It may prove hard ... O'Collins, *The Lord's Prayer*, p. 30.

the most important religious event since the Reformation ... Carl Jung, *Answer to Job*, translated by R. F. C. Hull (Oxford: Princeton University Press, 1958), p. 102.

CHAPTER 5

He is in heaven ... Karl Barth, *Prayer*, translated by W. L. Jenkins (Louisville, KY: Westminster John Knox Press, 2002), p. 26.

God's transcendence is demonstrated ... Barth, *Prayer*, p. 25.

lest there should be ... Thomas Aquinas, quoted by Paul Murray, *Praying with Confidence: Aquinas on the Lord's Prayer* (London: Continuum, 2010), p. 31.

because our final happiness ... Murray, *Praying with Confidence*, p. 32.

CHAPTER 6

This name is holiness ... Simone Weil, *Waiting on God*, translated by Emma Craufurd (London: Routledge & Kegan Paul Ltd, 1951), p. 146.

PART 2

The end and purpose ... Barth, *Prayer*, p. 35.

CHAPTER 7

Father, let ... See *The New Greek-English Interlinear New Testament*, trans. Brown and Comfort, p. 251.

You come against me ... Interview in Democracy Now: https://www.democracynow.org/2015/7/3/this_flag_comes_down_today_bree (accessed 6 September 2020).

CHAPTER 11

Kin-dom ... See Ada María Isasi-Díaz, *Mujerista Theology* (Maryknoll, MI: Orbis Books, 1996), pp. 88–92.

God's in his heaven— ... Robert Browning, 'Pippa's Song' (in *The Oxford Book of English Verse: 1250–1900*, ed. Arthur Quiller-Couch, 1919).

PART 3

There is no competition ... Leonardo Boff, *The Lord's Prayer: The Prayer of Integral Liberation*, translated by Theodore Morrow (Maryknoll, MI: Orbis Books, 1985), p. 74.

CHAPTER 13

food for all forms of growth ... Neil Douglas-Klotz, *Prayers of the Cosmos* (San Francisco, CA: HarperCollins, 1994), p. 26.

It often happens ... Murray, *Praying with Confidence*, p. 68.

CHAPTER 14

So we say ... Gregory of Nyssa, *The Lord's Prayer, The Beatitudes*, pp. 63–4.

the loveliness ... Gregory of Nyssa, *The Lord's Prayer, The Beatitudes*, p. 64.

Nature's flavouring ... Gregory of Nyssa, *The Lord's Prayer, The Beatitudes*, p. 67.

Give Thou bread ... Gregory of Nyssa, *The Lord's Prayer, The Beatitudes*, p. 67.

CHAPTER 15

For a collection of ancient English versions of the Lord's Prayer, see Nicholas Ayo, *The Lord's Prayer* (Oxford: Rowman & Littlefield, 1992).

What certain writers ... John Calvin, *Institutes of the Christian Religion*, translated by Ford Lewis Battles (Philadelphia: The Westminster Press, 1960), Book 3, chapter 20, paragraph 44, p. 908.

CHAPTER 17

food, drink, clothes ... Karl Barth, *Prayer*, p. 47.

nothing hinders us from ... Barth, Prayer, p. 47.

Bread is the mysterious ... Barth, Prayer, p. 48.

Give us this minimum ... Barth, *Prayer*, p. 49.

CHAPTER 18

what is in our hand ... Calvin, *Institutes*, Book 3, chapter 20, paragraph 44, p. 909.

PART 4

Forgiveness, forgiveness ... Pope Francis, *Our Father: Reflections on the Lord's Prayer* (London: Rider, 2017), p. 82.

CHAPTER 20

still trembling ... Sue Atkinson, *Struggling to Forgive: Moving on from trauma* (Oxford: Monarch Books, 2014), p. 32.

Jesus won't forgive... etc. Atkinson, *Struggling to Forgive*, pp. 38–9.

And when the perpetrators ... Miriam Toews, *Women Talking* (New York: Bloomsbury, 2018), p. 5.

We have to forgive ... Donald B. Kraybill, Steven M. Nolt and David L. Weaver-Zercher, *Amish Grace: How Forgiveness Transcended Tragedy* (San Francisco, CA: Jossey Bass, 2010), p. 51.

CHAPTER 21

For a collection of ancient English versions of the Lord's Prayer, see Nicholas Ayo, *The Lord's Prayer* (Oxford: Rowman & Littlefield, 1992).

CHAPTER 23

Finally, we petition ... Calvin, *Institutes*, Book 3, chapter 20, paragraph 45, p. 912.

For this reason ... Calvin, *Institutes*, Book 3, chapter 20, paragraph 45, p. 912.

If we retain ... Calvin, *Institutes*, Book 3, chapter 20, paragraph 45, p. 912.

CHAPTER 24

What God's forgiveness ... Barth, *Prayer*, p. 56.

the one who remains ... Maximus Confessor, *Selected Writings*, translated by George C. Berthold (Mahwah, NJ: Paulist Press, 1985), p. 115.

a pure disposition ... Maximus, *Selected Writings*, p. 116.

It says Jesus ... Marilynne Robinson, *Gilead* (London: Virago: 2004), p. 183.

we are not faced ... Barth, *Prayer*, p. 55.

PART 5

The prayer began with the word ... Weil, *Waiting on God*, p. 152.

CHAPTER 25

we should be separated from ... Gregory of Nyssa, *The Lord's Prayer, The Beatitudes*, p. 83.

CHAPTER 26

prayer to be spared ... John Nolland, *The Gospel of Matthew* (Bletchley: The Paternoster Press, 2005), p. 292.

CHAPTER 27

But God tries ... Calvin, *Institutes*, Book 3, chapter 20, paragraph 46, p. 913.

PART 6

Glory is the final word of religion ... Evelyn Underhill, *Abba* (London: Longmans, Green and Co., 1940), p. 85.

CHAPTER 31

Solemn exclamation ... Alexander Schmemann, see *Our Father*, translated by Alexis Vinogradov (New York: St Vladimir's Seminary Press, 2002), pp. 88–9.

For Thine is the Kingdom ... Olivier Clément, *Three Prayers*, translated by Michael Breck (New York: St Vladimir's Seminary Press, 2000), p. 41.

'These words, Kingdom, Power, and Glory, ... Lancelot Andrewes, *Works*, *Sermons*, Volume Five. *Certain Sermons Preached at Sundry Times upon Several Occasions*, transcribed by Marianne Dorman, 'The Lord's Prayer Sermon XVIII', p. 463; http://anglicanhistory.org/lact/andrewes/v5/prayer18.html (accessed 13 June 2020).

If we consider ... Lancelot Andrewes, *Works*, transcribed by Marianne Dorman, 'The Lord's Prayer Sermon XVIII', p. 463; http://anglicanhistory.org/lact/andrewes/v5/prayer18.html (accessed 13 June 2020).

CHAPTER 33

All of us believe ... Michelle Obama, *Becoming* (London: Viking, 2018), p. 383.

You belong ... Michelle Obama, *Becoming*, p. 384.

CHAPTER 34

'deep down things' ... From Gerard Manley Hopkins' poem 'God's Grandeur', which is widely anthologized.

Thine is the Glory ... Underhill, *Abba*, p. 84.

God is the interesting thing ... The letter from Evelyn Underhill to Cosmo Gordon Lang, Archbishop of

Canterbury, was found among her papers after she died. It is available online at http://www.anglicanlibrary.org/underhill/UnderhillLettertoArchbishopLangofCanterbury.pdf (accessed 18 June 2020).

Absolute Beauty ... Underhill, *Abba*, pp. 84–5.
divine glory ... Black, *The Lord's Prayer*, p. 240.
Glory is ... Underhill, *Abba*, p. 85.

CHAPTER 36

We should ask ... Weil, *Waiting on God*, p. 149.